# ELECTRICITY THEFT: EMPOWERING PEOPLE AND REFORMING POWER SECTOR

# Electricity Theft: Empowering People and Reforming Power Sector

SURINDER KUMAR

INSTITUTE FOR DEVELOPMENT AND COMMUNICATION

MANOHAR
2004

First published 2004



ISBN 81-7304-530-5

*Published by*
Ajay Kumar Jain for
Manohar Publishers & Distributors
4753/23 Ansari Road, Daryaganj
New Delhi 110 002

*Typeset by*
Kohli Print
Delhi 110 051

*Printed at*
Lordson Publishers Pvt. Ltd.
New Delhi 110 007

# Contents

# Tables

# Preface

Electricity is the most versatile form of energy. Its adequate supply is essential for the socio-economic development of any present-day society. Being a highly capital-intensive product, the investment resource requirement to meet the growing electricity demand has been, at times, beyond the means of the developing countries. Tied 'aid' from the multilateral lending institutions has its own consequences. Large amounts of scarce capital resources have already been sunk in the electricity supply industry. However, its financial performance has been highly unsatisfactory. Unless adequate internal resource generation is ensured, the financial crisis in the daily operations as well as the further expansion of the electric power system cannot be resolved. The restroration of the financial health of the electric power system warrants the undertaking of a number of measures.

With the introduction of the new economic policy in India since 1991, the power sector was the first public sector industry where reforms were attempted and are still in the progress. The State Electricity Boards are the major agencies responsible for the generation, transmission, and distribution of electricity in India. Piferage of power or power theft has turned out to be one of the major factors for the non-realization of adequate revenue from the sale of electricity. As pilferage is very closely linked with the administrative and management practices being followed today, this theft of power is like a cancer that is eating into their vitals. In the past, a number of technical solutions like installing tamper-proof meters and boxes were adopted but the culprits remain a step ahead. Second, as experience has revealed even the best-intentioned rules in the law books do not mean much unless the enforcing agency and the society at large possess the required will and commitment to honour them. One of the major planks of the power sector reforms is the privatization of the distribution of electricity. It has been noted that privatization per se will not solve these long-festering problems. Pilferage of power in India has become a social menace. It has been highly institutionalized. Breaking the nexus will require, along with technical solutions a number of changes in the organization management practices, and a shift in the attitude of the people towards public goods. To achieve all this social marketing strategies need to be devised. This book analyses the institutional dynamics of these issues and an effort is made here to provide social solutions to the problems.

In this book I have drawn on material from a number of research studies conducted earlier by me. Two projects, namely, 'Electricity Theft and Conservation of Power in Punjab' (1996) sponsored by the Punjab State Electricity Board through the Institute for Development and Communication, Chandigarh and 'Financial Performance and Pricing Policy: Haryana State Electricity Board' (1998) sponsored by the Indian Council of Social Science Research, New Delhi have provided the basis for the book. The entire data and discussion have been updated in the light of recent experience.

Dr Promod Kumar, Director Institute for Development and Communication Chandigarh and Mr R.N. Gupta, former Chairman, Punjab State Electricity Board, Patiala provided theoretical inputs in formulating the issues in relation to the pilferage of power. My colleague Dr Rajender Chaudhary carefully and painstakingly read and reread various drafts of this manuscript, questioned some of my formulations, and helped me avoid many pitfalls both of logic and style. Mr D.K. Joshi, Deputy Chief (Economics), Central Electricity Regulatory Commission, New Delhi, Dr Atul Sood, Senior Economist, and Dr Navsharan G. Singh, Senior Economist, National Council of Applied Economic Research New Delhi, made many constructive suggestions in the final draft. I gratefully acknowledge their contribution to the study.

I record with sincere thanks the active cooperation extended by Dr P.N. Sharma, Librarian, Maharshi Dayanand University, Rohtak and his staff; and the research team, in particular Mr Vinod Kumar, Mr Ashok Kumar, and Mr Ravinder Singh, staff of the data processing unit, and the librarian of the Institute for Development and Communication, all of whom enthusiastically provided the help required in preparing this book. The support of Mr Sunil Kumar, my Ph.D. student, in carrying out a number of odd jobs, including the updating of the tables, is highly appreciated.

I sincerely express my gratitude to Lt. Gen. B.S. Suhag, the Vice-Chancellor, Maharshi Dayanand University, Rohtak for promptly sanctioning me the much needed one-year sabbatical leave, thus freeing me from routine teaching work to enable me to pursue the latest studies to bring myself up to date with developments in the field and thus to finish this book. Last put not the least, I acknowledge the contribution of my wife Dr Sunita Sharma and our children Abhinav and Anupriya who 'exempted' me from household responsibilities, thus affording me the opportunity to fully devote myself to my academic pursuits.

*Rohtak*
*15 September 2003*

SURINDER KUMAR

# Glossary

## ACRONYMS

| | | |
|---|---|---|
| ARR | : | Annual Revenue Requirement |
| HERC | : | Haryana Electricity Regulatory Authority |
| HSEB | : | Haryana State Electricity Board |
| HVPNL | : | Haryana Vidyut Prasaran Nigam Limited |
| UHBVNL | : | Uttar Haryana Bijli Vitran Nigam Limited |
| DHBVNL | : | Dakshin Haryana Bijli Vitran Nigam Limited |
| PSEB | : | Punjab State Electricity Board |
| GDP | : | Gross Domestic Product |
| KW | : | Kilowatt = 1,000 watt |
| MW | : | Megawatt = 1,000,000 watt |
| KWh | : | Kilowatt hour = one unit of electric energy |
| MU | : | Million Units = Million KWh |
| O&M | : | Operation and Maintenance |

## NON-ENGLISH UNITS AND WORDS

1 Lakh = 100,000
1 Crore = 100 lakhs = 10 million = 10,000,000
1 Paisa = One-hundredth of a Rupee
Rs. = Rupees

Gross operating surplus/deficit: Operating surplus or deficit (gross) before providing for depreciation and interest to the institutions and to the state government, i.e. revenue receipts less operating expenses.

Commercial profit/loss: Net surplus/deficit, i.e. gross operating surplus or deficit less depreciation, interest due to institutional creditors and to the state government, i.e. total revenue minus total cost.

Capital base: Original costs of fixed assets in service reduced by cumulative depreciation and consumer's contribution for service lines at the beginning of the year. It is also known as net assets at the beginning of the year.

Average tariff: Average rate of realization of revenue from sale of energy, i.e. revenue from sale divided by units sold.

Average cost: Total cost, i.e. revenue expenditure plus depreciation and interest due, divided by total electricity sold.

Revenue receipts: Revenue from sale of energy plus miscellaneous revenue receipts, like subsidy/subvention and other receipts.

Effective subsidy: The amount actually lost by the SEBs on account of sale of electricity at less than average cost to a sector, i.e. average cost minus average tariff times the number of units sold to a given sector.

Rate of return (ROR): Rate of commercial profits/losses to net fixed assets, expressed as a percentage.

CHAPTER 1

# Introduction

India achieved political freedom from the British colonial rulers on 15 August 1947 after a prolonged struggle. During the struggle for independence, the masses were full of enthusiasm and saw a ray of hope for their economic emancipation in achieving freedom from foreign rule. To meet the aspirations of the people and fired by the idealism generated in the course of the freedom struggle, the national political leadership was keen to follow a path of accelerated economic development. Rapid industrialization with social justice emerged as the key economic blueprint championed by the new ruling elite. To accelerate the pace of industrialization, the country required a comprehensive infrastructure network, basic and heavy industries, and an assured supply of energy. These industries required large amounts of capital investment, had a long gestation period, and the returns were subject to a high degree of risk and uncertainty. The profit-maximizing private industrialists did not necessarily opt for such kinds of investments. However these industries were a prerequisite for laying the foundation of the economic base of an independent India. The Mahalanobis model of development provided a theoretical basis for a self-reliant development strategy. The government at that time, therefore, rightly took upon itself the task of developing these industries. The public sector was assigned a very important role in this regard.

Prime Minister Jawaharlal Nehru opted for a mixed economic model of development. The vision of the 1950s was that the country could achieve a peaceful social revolution to establish a socialistic pattern of society without the interruption caused by drastic changes in the basic institutions. To achieve self-reliance, the Mahalanobis strategy was adopted, but without land reforms which he had advocated as a necessary complement to the programme of economic development. Despite significant achievements in bringing about self-reliance between 1950 and 1990, structural constraints and the deepening balance of payment crisis provided the ostensible grounds for the government to reconsider its development strategy. One alternative was to undertake institutional reforms, especially in agriculture in the regions having a semi-feudal social structure as in Bihar, Orissa, eastern Uttar Pradesh, and Madhya Pradesh. This would have increased agricultural production, as well as income in the hands of the poor people, which in turn would have created an increase in the demand for essential industrial consumer goods, alleviating poverty, on the one hand, and pulling the essential industries out of recession, on the other. But the government yielded to internal and external pressures of various vested interests and decided to follow another set of policies. After contributing a great deal to the achievement of self-reliance, the public sector became the victim of vested interests of the political leadership and the bureaucracy. The public sector could have been restored to health by restructuring public enterprise management and ensuring relative autonomy along with accountability and transparency. However, the political leadership and the bureaucracy decided to follow what is popularly known as the International Monetary Fund-World Bank-sponsored development strategy.

Since 1991, the Government of India has embarked on a new economic policy consisting of: (a) the stabilization of the economy; (b) its restructuring; and (c) a path of growth based on the policy of the liberalization, privatization, and globalization of the Indian economy and an export-led growth based on international demand and supply. Many intellectuals, particularly Third World intellectuals, have strong reservations regarding the wisdom of this development philosophy and the consequent strategy based on it.[1]

Consistent with the new economic policy, one of the first public sectors to undertake restructuring in the process of reforms was the electric power sector. Power sector reforms were initiated in October 1991. Whether by design of default, the power sector investment plan in the Eighth Five Year Plan (1992–7) became a casualty of the reforms process. The Central Electricity Authority (CEA) had projected a requirement of an additional 48,000 MW power-generating capacity during the Eighth Five Year Plan. The Planning Commission's Working Group on Power, set up in September 1991, recommended an addition of 36,645.7 MW. However, because of resource constraints the Eighth Plan provided resources for 30,538 MW. During the Plan period, the central and state governments sharply reduced the budgetary support to power projects and the Plan target was further scaled down to 20,729 MW on the ground of resource constraints. The actual addition to the generating capacity during the Eighth Plan was a mere 16,422.4 MW. Obviously, the state abdicated its responsibility to provide adequate resources for planned investment to add to the generating capacity as per the five year plan. These tactics appeared to be aimed at creating a fear of financial crisis to provide legitimacy to the privatization process.

The Indian Electricity Act, 1910, the Electricity (Supply) Act, 1948, and the Indian Electricity Rules, 1956 have been amended; the Electricity Laws (Amendment) Act, 1998 and the Electricity Regulatory Commission Act, 1998 provide the framework for the regulation of electricity and incorporate new legal, administrative, and financial provisions to allow and encourage private participation in the power sector. Private and foreign companies have been provided a number of extra market incentives to attract investment in this sector. The private companies are provided a 16 per cent assured rate of return on their equity and a 0.7 per cent additional return for every 1 per cent increase in the plant load factor (PLF) over the 68.5 per cent level. For assured returns, the state government will provide a guarantee and under certain conditions the central government will give a counter guarantee. Foreign equity return will be in foreign currency and will be completely protected against foreign exchange rate fluctuations. Other concessions include an enhanced rate of depreciation at 7.5 per cent and a tax holiday.[2] A comprehensive 'Electricity Bill 2001' has been passed by the Parliament on 5 May 2003 after a long and protracted debate in the country. The new Act wil replace all the existing laws relating to the electricity supply industry.

The present strategy of power sector reforms consists of the unbundling of vertically integrated State Electricity Boards (SEBs) into separate generation, transmission, and distribution corporations, the establishment of Electricity Regulatory Commissions, the removal of all subsidies and cross subsidies, and ultimately the privatization of the generation, transmission, and distribution of electricity. There has been a lot of controversy over the validity as well as the desirability of unbundling the electric power system and its privatization. Academics, professionals and policy makers are engaged in a heated debate on the issue. It has also been argued that the existing laws governing electricity supply in India are adequate. Only problem is the lack of political will to enforce the existing laws. Privatization *per se* does not provide the solution to the real problems faced by electric power systems in India. The key problem is not on the generation side. The main problem relates to the distribution of electricity and realization of revenue. A major reason for the poor financial performance of the SEBs is the irrational pricing policy, pilferage of power and subsidization policy without accountability. An alternative strategy could be to establish separate generation, transmission, and distribution corporations; ensure their professional management with a commercial outlook and guarantee them autonomy from government; ensure internal generation of revenue by following a rational pricing policy and by the elimination of pilferage of power; and also establish independent Electricity Regulatory Commissions to oversee the functioning of the electric power system.[3] One of the major problems, which has been eating into the vitalities of the technical and financial health of the state electricity utilities, is the problem of power theft. To be in a position to appreciate the problem and its intricacies, we shall have to examine the problem as it evolved from a historical perspective.

The patronage exercised by the political and powerful socio-economic classes over a long period of time has made the rampant pilferage of electric power a social menace. It has been institutionalized to such an extent that it does not attract any social antipathy or protest. Though technical solutions to the problem may be available, unscrupulous elements always find ways and means to frustrate administrative as well as technical measures. Various attempts to overcome this problem have proved to be inadequate and ineffective. Legal and technical measures must be complemented by effective social intervention strategies to achieve a reasonable level of success. Keeping these facts in view, an attempt has been made in this book to undertake in-depth analysis of the problem of the pilferage of power or power theft with a focus on its social dynamics. An analysis of the electric power investment planning, as well as the technical and financial performances of the main agencies of electricity generation, transmission and distribution in India—the SEBs—provides the point of departure for this study.

Electricity is the most versatile form of energy. Electric power was accorded high priority in India's five year plans. The share of the energy sector in the total Plan outlay in all the five year plans was about 30 per cent and more than two-thirds of it was allocated to electric power. The total generation capacity at the time of India's Independence in 1947 was 1,370 MW. It increased to more than

97,846 MW by 31 March 2000. The installed generating capacity in the utility sector now exceeds 100,000 MW. In addition to it, there is about 20,000 MW of captive generation capacity in the private sector. During the period 1947–2000, the generating capacity in the utility sector increased at the annual rate of about 8.4 per cent and the energy generated increased about 10 per cent per annum. An increase of more than 70 times in the generating capacity over a period of fifty years is indeed a great achievement. The Indian electric power system is predominantly a mix of hydro power (24 per cent) and thermal power (72 per cent). The contribution of nuclear power is about 3 per cent and of wind power 1 per cent.[4]

Despite a very impressive expansion of the electric power system, it is faced with a number of technical as well as financial problems. The demand for electric power continued to outstrip the supply throughout the last three decades. The SEBs resorted to load shedding, which hampered industrial as well as agricultural production. The overall energy shortage was about 6.2 per cent and the peak shortage about 12.4 per cent in 1999–2000. Two major factors responsible for poor technical performance of the Indian electric power system are the low level of capacity utilization of the thermal plants managed mostly by the SEBs and high transmission and distribution (T&D) losses which reportedly range between 21 and 26 per cent in the country.[5]

The SEBs are facing a serious financial crisis and are not in a position to generate the required amount of financial resources for further expansion. As per section 59 of the Electricity (Supply) Act, 1948, the SEBs are required to earn a minimum return of not less than 3 per cent on their fixed assets after fully meeting the fixed and operating costs, interest, and tax liabilities.[6] The political leadership of the state governments as well as the managements of the SEBs, which are generally administered and controlled by the state bureaucracy, never bother to honour this statutory obligation. Political leaders indulge in competitive populism and try to appease their electoral constituencies by directing the SEBs to supply electricity at subsidized rates or free of cost without any valid socio-economic rationale, thus landing these utilities into a financial crisis. The aggregate commercial losses of the SEBs in 2000–1 were estimated to be Rs. 24,237 crore and they are expected to increase to Rs. 28,445 crore in 2001–2. Estimated gross subsidy to agricultural consumers in 2001–2 is about Rs. 29,461 crore and to domestic consumers,

Rs. 11,267 crore.[7] Such high levels of commercial losses are not sustainable by the economy. In January 2001 the SEBs owed Rs. 28,939 crore to the central power utilities like the National Thermal Power Corporation (NTPC) and Rs. 13,971 crore to central sector companies outside the power sector like the Railways.[8] The external sources of financing the power sector from within the country have dwindled over time. Foreign borrowings, especially from the multilateral financial institutions, have visible as well as invisible strings attached to them, which have serious implications for the national economy.[9] At the same time, the cost of electric supply is an overestimate inflated by inefficiencies. A valid question is: Why should genuine consumers be made to pay for the inefficiencies of the SEBs? The electricity sales to the agricultural and domestic sectors is about half of the total sale, whereas the revenue realized from these sectors is one-sixth of the total sale revenue. The state governments do not fully compensate the SEBs for the subsidized supply, thus landing the SEBs in deep financial crises. The culture of unaccountability, thus engendered and encouraged, permeates the whole institutional framework and the consequent contagion of gross inefficiency paralyses the entire system. The system could be spared such avoidable chaos if government interference were kept to the minimum and if the SEBs were allowed to function as autonomous commercial-cum-service corporations as required by the Electricity (Supply) Act.[10]

To overcome the problems of the power sector, the Government of India has, since 1991, made a number of amendments to the laws regulating the electricity supply industry in India. These changes have long-term consequences. It has been argued that in the process of restructuring, corporatization is expected to lead to commercialization in its functioning and operations. However, this may not take place because the government will either remain the sole owner or the majority shareholder of the restructured companies. The corporatized electric supply utilities will have a fair chance of functioning in a commercially viable manner only when the government stops interfering in the day-to-day administration of the electric supply utilities, avoids compromises on commercial norms, or fully compensates the commercial losses suffered by these utilities for meeting mandated subsidies. Questions are also being raised whether the SEBs will be reformed if state governments are bribed to carry out such reforms.[11] Will the policy of extending loans on soft terms and conditions induce the SEBs to improve their technical and financial performance? Past experience shows that conditional lending does not work unless the borrowing entity genuinely wants, for its own autonomous reasons, to implement the package of conditions that accompanies the loan. When such motivation is missing, the borrower finds various devious means to take the money on offer and yet not implement the conditions, securing which is the lender's objective. It often happens that such lending programmes are discontinued after the first few tranches of funds are released and it is discovered that the borrower has failed to implement the conditions agreed to. Even the conditional lending by the central government to the states is not likely to produce different results.[12]

The SEBs are supposed to be autonomous corporations, but past experience suggests that their actual position is no better than that of a state government department. They are overstaffed and are plagued with low productivity levels. There is a general lack of professional management in matters of commitment, accountability, and initiative in decision making. The individuals occupying management positions change frequently according to the compulsions of political expediency. The chairpersons are generally state bureacrats who lack adequate professional knowledge or accountability and commitment to the utility. The tenures of chairpersons and chief engineers are not fixed and these are very short. Appointments on political considerations or seniority induces a lack of commitment and involvement in serious policy-making. There is widespread nepotism and favouritism at the cost of merit.[13] What the system badly requires is essence-specific reforms, not structure-specific reforms. Unless reforms ensure transparency, accountability, and improved performance of the restructured companies, they shall not succeed. The edifice of political patronage, corruption, and inefficiency needs to be demolished.

There can be no two opinions that the existing energy resources should be efficiently managed, but the prevalent economic paradigm is highly energy intensive and is not really sustainable over the long run. In fact, one of the key issues before human kind is to ensure the adequate supply of energy without posing such threats to the environment as have already begun to endanger its very existence. Fossil fuels (coal, petroleum, and natural gas) account for about 88 per cent of the total energy consumed in the world. Gases emitted during the burning of fossil fuel can degrade the environment, perhaps to the extent of drastically altering the climate and threatening the future habitability of the planet. Second, at the present rate of depletion, fossil fuels may not last beyond a hundred years. Therefore, global efforts are being made to search for renewable and clean sources of energy. Third, as the existing energy-use pattern is unsustainable, demand-side management through the efficient use of the existing sources of energy and conservation of energy are the main planks of the alternative paradigm being advocated to make future economic development environmentally sustainable.[14] From this perspective, solutions to the problems of efficient use of energy, reduction of transmission and distribution losses, avoiding wastage, reducing the pilferage of electric power, and increasing conservation of electric energy have become all the more important from the social viewpoint.

## TRANSMISSION AND DISTRIBUTION LOSSES

In the process of transmission and distribution of electricity to the consumers, part of the electricity is dissipated and/or lost. This loss of energy has two components: technical losses; and non-technical losses. Technical losses consist of the energy dissipated in transmission and distribution wires, controlling switchgears, and transformation equipment used in the system to supply power to the consumers. Technical loss can be measured and their reduction requires technical solutions to improve the efficiency of the transmission and distribution network. They may include reducing the number of joints, replacing worn-out lines reducing loads on the existing lines, improving the efficiency of transformers and augmenting their capacity by new additions, installing capacitors for reactive compensation and for improving the voltage profile, etc.

Non-technical losses are due to pilferage of power, defective meters, errors in meter reading and/or unmetered supply, etc. Pilferage of power or power theft may broadly be defined as the dishonest use of electric energy by any person (including authorized or legal consumers) by either bypassing the meters completely or by tampering with them in such a manner that they do not record the consumption fully or record it only partly. Non-technical losses represent that part of electricity which is consumed but not billed, whereby the utility or the electricity board incurs financial losses in its operation. Thus,

Non-technical losses = Total measured losses – Measured technical losses

= [Net generation – Billed sale] – Measured technical losses

Since non-technical losses represent such consumption of electricity as is not paid for, i.e. consumed free, it has a serious aggravating effect on increasing conspicuous consumption and demand. This rising demand, in turn, could aggravate technical losses. If pilferage coincides with the peak system demand, it exerts pressure on the installed capacity, which may require further expansion (and investment) to meet the increased demand. Thus, non-technical losses represent an economic cost to society as well as a financial loss to the electricity board or utility, and genuine consumers may have to pay more for their electricity consumption.

Estimates of T&D losses in India are at best intelligent guesses as most of the states provide significant amount of electricity supply which is unmetered, particularly to the agricultural sector. It becomes difficult to determine the extent of pilferage. In the 1990s, T&D losses were reported to be between 19.8 per cent and 24.4 per cent per annum.[15] The internationally accepted norm for T&D losses is 7 per cent to 10 per cent. The Centre for Monitoring of Indian Economy (CMIE) has estimated that 12 per cent to 15 per cent T&D losses are acceptable in Indian conditions. The CEA has laid 15 per cent loss as the acceptable norm. The Eighth Five Year Plan has targeted to bring down T&D losses by 5 per cent at the rate of 1 per cent per annum. The emphasis on reduction in T&D losses continuses to be featured in the Ninth Plan as well.

It is a well-known fact that the official estimates of T&D losses conceal more than what they reveal. It has been reported that T&D losses in some of the states are between 30 per cent and 50 per cent of the total electricity supply. Most of the electricity which may be pilfered by industrial, agricultural, domestic, or commercial consumers is shown as a part of agricultural consumption or unmetered supply. Official estimates of agricultural consumption in published accounts are more of a policy decision than they are true estimates. When corruption becomes rampant, there is no incentive for the employees to improve their efficiency as it may not be recognized or rewarded, and the management becomes unresponsive to market signals. The consumers are also encouraged to indulge in pilferage of power, as they have no fear of being punished.

The problem of power theft has many dimensions. Pilferage of power leads primarily to financial losses to the SEBs. The loss of revenue, when electricity is consumed by not paid for by some consumers, imposes a heavy burden on the financial viability of the utilities, directly as well as indirectly. In fact, the situation has become all the more alarming as most of the SEBs are already on the verge of financial bankruptcy. They do not have the required funds for investment to expand the generation, transmission, and distribution systems, as well as to take steps to reduce technical losses by introducing T&D loss reduction devices.

To have an assessment of the financial loss caused by power theft, an illustrative example will be quite illuminating. For the year 1999–2000, it has been estimated that gross energy generation by the utilities was 480.7 billion units. Taking the Planning Commission's estimates of auxiliary consumption as 10.15 per cent, energy available for sale was 431.89 billion units, and estimated T&D losses were 22 per cent. As has been stated, in Indian conditions T&D losses should not be more than 15 per cent. A reduction in the loss by 7 per cent would have saved 30.23 billion units sold at Rs. 2.076 per unit (the average tariff rate for the year 1999–2000) and this would have generated Rs. 6,276 crore in the year which would have been adequate to install about 2,000 MW of additional generating capacity.[16]

Such a situation, where the utility follow neither the principles of private corporate management nor the social accountability principles of the public sector, is bound to lead to the collapse of the utility.

Power theft is a cognizable offence and cases are booked under section 39 and section 44 of the Indian Electricity Act, 1910. If a person or consumer indulges in theft of power, this crime is punishable with imprisonment for a term which may extend to three year, or with a fine which is not less than one thousand rupees, or with both. Section 44 provides penalty for interference with meters or licensee's works and for improper use of energy. Punishment under section 44 is imprisonment for a term which may extend to three years or with a fine which may extend to five thousand rupees or with both.[17] Though legal provisions appear quite strict, they have not proved to be effective in practice.

## OBJECTIVES AND PLAN OF THE STUDY

We have discussed in the preceding sections that the problem of pilferage of power in India has been highly institutionalized. No power section reforms involving only restructuring, including privatization, will prove to be adequate to satisfactorily resolve the problem of power theft. It has been noted that even the best of laws when not enforced are reduced to the status of paper tigers. The most sophisticated and foolproof metering system will not achieve the desired results if the management, the meter-reading staff, and the consumers actively connive. In such a situation, any reforms process which affects the vested interests will be scuttled and hence made infructuous. A recent example is the resistance of the employees to the installation of interface metering equipment at the grid sub-stations, and the replacement of traditional meters by electronic meters at the consumer's end from the commercial and domestic consumers. There is a strong, organized resistance to meter supply to private agricultural tube wells for accounting purpose, despite the assurance that the flat rate system and subsidized supply to agriculture shall continue. Disinformation campaigns and rumours about in the market that electronic meters are faster by, say, 30 per cent and that the distribution companies want to fleece the genuine consumers. In the prevailing environment, even the private distribution companies will not come forward, especially in the rural areas. This sorry state of affairs warrant the introduction of effective social solutions to the problem with a long-term strategy. Therefore, in this study we will examine various institutional and social aspects of the problem of pilferage of power and energy conservation with a view to developing a sound policy pacakage and intervention strategies to ensure high efficiency of management; combat the problem of power theft; improve the financial position of the SEBs in India; and improve consumer satisfaction.

As discussed in the preceding section, T&D losses have two component: technical losses and non-technical losses. This study is focused primarily on issues related to non-technical losses, which are mainly due to pilferage of power. Solutions to the problem of power theft have technical, administrative, and social aspects. Meters should be installed in tamper-proof boxes, meter checking should be made more effective and deterrent punishment be awarded, employees should be motivated, and the community should be involved in fighting this menace. However, effective solutions shall have to be developed through an objective understanding of the ground realities.

To place the problem of pilferage of electric power in the proper perspective, a review of the electric power systems in Punjab and Haryana has been carried out here. This includes both the technical as well as the financial performance of the Punjab State Electricity Board (PSEB) and the erstwhile Haryana State Electricity Board

(HSEB), categories of consumers, connected load and energy consumed by various categories of consumers, and structural changes therein over a period of time. An assessment of T&D losses over a period has been made and their implications analysed. The existing rules and procedures to check theft of power and their actual implementation have been examined.

As this study is focused on finding organizational, managerial, motivational, and community-oriented solutions to the problem of pilferage of power, the perceptions of the various categories of consumers as well as of the employees involved at different levels in the distribution of electricity in Punjab have been subjected to a detailed analysis. For this, a field survey was conducted and the perceptions of the consumers and the employees on the following aspects were recorded and analysed.

1. The perceptions of consumers and employees and their attitudes towards the problems of power theft and energy conservation.
2. Knowledge and use of various methods to pilfer power and methods to check it.
3. Perceptions regarding the relationship between pilferage of electricity and the existing tariff rates and the tariff structure.
4. Perceptions about the efficacy of the existing organizational structure, accountability, and responsiveness.
5. Nature and role of incentives, role of the employees' unions, additional powers, motivational steps, and nature of re-orientation and training programmes to be imparted to the employees.
6. Perceptions regarding community-based intervention strategies.

## ORGANIZATION OF THE BOOK

This book is organized into six chapters, including the introductory chapter. Chapter 2 contains, a review of the technical and financial performance of the PSEB over a twenty-year period, from 1975 to 1995. Chapter 3 consists of a review of the technical and financial performance of the erstwhile HSEB, since its formation in 1967 to 1998 when it was restructured. Chapter 4 deals with perceptions of respondent consumers regarding pilferage of power and conservation of energy. Chapter 5 describes the perceptions of respondent employees in this regard. Finally, Chapter 6 contains a summary of the report and the policy implications/recommendations arising therefrom.

## NOTES

1. Dalip S. Swamy, *The Political Economy of Industrialisation: From Self-Reliance to Globalisation*, New Delhi: Sage Publishers, 1994.
   Deepak Nayyar, *Economic Liberalisation in India: Analytics, Experience and Lessons*, Calcutta: Orient Longman, 1996.
   Amit Bhaduri and Deepak Nayyar, *The Intelligent Person's Guide to Liberalisation*, New Delhi: Penguin Books, 1996.
   Neeraj Jain, *Globalisation or Recolonisation*, Pune: Elgar, 2001.
   Michel Chossudovsky, *The Globalisation of Poverty: Impact of IMF and World Bank Reforms*, Penang: Third World Network, 1997.
2. Surinder Kumar, *'Power Sector' Alternative Economic Survey 1993–4*, New Delhi: Public Interest Research Group, 1994.
3. V. Balu, 'Issues and Challenges Concerning Privatization and Regulation in the Power Sector', *Energy for Sustainable Development*, Bangalore: IEI, 1997, pp. 6–13.
   Prabir Purkayastha and Arun Ghosh, *Current Power Sector Policies: A Need for a National Debate*, New Delhi: National Working Group on Power, 1998.
   Amulya K.N. Reddy, 'California Energy Crisis and the Lessons for Power Sector Reforms in India', *Economic and Political Weekly*, vol. 36 no. 18, May 2001, pp. 1533–40.
4. Planning Commission, *Annual Report on the Working of State Electricity Boards and Electricity Departments*, New Delhi, 2000, p. 26.
5. Government of India, *Economic Survey 2000–1*, New Delhi: Ministry of Finance, pp. 174–7.
6. Government of India, *The Electricity (Supply) Act, 1948*, New Delhi, 1996.
7. *Economic Survey 2000–1*, p. 176.
8. T.L. Shankar, *Fiscal Impact of Electricity Boards Overdues on State's Finances*, Hyderabad: Administraive Staff College of India, 2001.
9. P. Purakayastha, 'New Power Policy: Bankrupting the Power Sector', *Economic and Political Weekly*, vol. 28, no. 20, May 1993, p. 955.
   Sebastian Morris, 'Political Economy of Power Sector in India', *Economic and Political Weekly*, 18–25 May 1996, pp. 1274–86.
10. K.P. Kannan, N. Vijayamohanan Pillai, 'Plight of Power Sector in India-II: Financial Performance of SEBs', *Economic and Political Weekly*, vol. 36, no. 3, 20–6 January 2001, pp. 234–6.
11. V. Balu, op. cit., pp. 6–13.
12. *Economic and Political Weekly*, Editorial, 'Power Reforms: Market Structure, the Key', vol. 36, no. 10, 10–16 March 2001, p. 796.
13. K.P. Kannan and N. Vijayamohanan Pillai, 'Plight of Power Sector in India-I: Physical Performance of SEBs', *Economic and Political Weekly*, vol. 36, no. 2, 13–19, January 2001, pp. 130–9.

14. J. Goldernberg, et al., *Energy for Sustainable World*, New Delhi: Wiley Eastern 1988.
    Amulya Kumar N. Reddy et al. 'Development-Focused End-Use-Oriented Electricity Scenario for Karnataka', *Economic and Policial Weekly*, vol. 26, no. 14, 6 April 1991, pp. 891–910, and vol. 26, no. 15, 13 April 1991, pp. 983–1004.
    A. Gadgil and G. Jannuzzi, 'Conservation Potential of Compact Fluorescent Lamps in India and Brazil', *Energy Policy*, vol. 19, no. 6, 1991, pp. 449–63.
    National Productivity Council, *Report on Review of Power End-Use Efficiencies*, New Delhi, 1991.
15. Ibid., Planning Commission, 2000, p. 66.
16. Calcultaotins are based on data from the *Annual Report on the Working of the State Electricity Boards and Electricity Departments* (April 2000), pp. 65–6 and 133, and *Economic Survey 2000–1*, Table S-29.
17. The Indian Electricity Act, 1910.

CHAPTER 2

# Performance of the Punjab State Electricity Board

In the previous chapter we discussed some vital emerging issues of India's electric-power sector. It has been noted that in the process of electric supply, the transmission and distribution losses are at an unacceptably high proportion of the total energy supply. One of the key components of the T&D losses is the pilferage of power. To provide a perspective on this issue and to comprehend it in all its dimensions, the technical and financial performance of two State Electricity Boards, namely, the Punjab State Electricity Board (PSEB) and the erstwhile Haryana State Electricity Board (HSEB) has been subjected to a detailed analysis in the next two chapters. In this chapter, the technical and financial performance of the PSEB in the last two decades and some related issues are examined. This chapter is divided into four sections.

Section 1 deals with the growth and performance of the generation, transmission, and distribution systems in Punjab. Section 2 reviews the financial position of the PSEB. Section 3 deals with the transmission and distribution losses in Punjab. Section 4 discusses the extent of power theft in Punjab and examines the remedial measures taken by the PSEB.

## 1. GENERATION, TRANSMISSION, AND DISTRIBUTION SYSTEMS IN PUNJAB

The PSEB was constituted on 1 February 1959 under section 5(i) of the Electricity (Supply) Act, 1948. Subsequently, the erstwhile state of Punjab was reorganized under the State's Reorganisation Act, 1966, and the electricity board in its present form came into being on 2 May 1967.

As Punjab does not own natural resources of energy like coal and petroleum, the development of electric power was accorded a very high priority in its planned economic development. The share of the power sector outlay in the total Plan outlay in Punjab from the Fifth Five Year Plan to the Ninth Five Year Plan is presented in Table 2.1. It may be noted that up to the Eighth Five Year Plan, the share of the power sector in the total Plan outlay ranged between 35 per cent and 50 per cent which is quite high. However, the outlay in the Ninth Five Year Plan has been significantly reduced to 26 per cent, which indicates that the state government has reduced its commitment to develop the power sector.

Punjab has a mixed electric power system consisting of hydro and thermal power plants. The total installed generating capacity as on 31 March 1999 was 3,964 MW, which consisted of 1,844 MW (46.5 per cent) of hydro and 2,120 MW (53.5 per cent) of thermal power. The state has a vast transmission and distribution network. The lengths of the various transmission and distribution lines as on 21 March 1999 were: 3,374 km of 220 KV lines, 2,948 km of 132 KV lines, 4,045 km of 66 KV lines, 1,560 km of 33 KV lines, 85,572 km of 11 KV lines, and 151,615 km of Low Tension (LT) lines.[1]

The installed electricity-generating capacity of the PSEB for the

TABLE 2.1: SHARE OF POWER SECTOR IN PLAN OUTLAY

*(Rs. in crore)*

| Period | Total Plan Outlay | Power Sector Outlay | Share of Power Sector Outlay in Total Outlay % |
|---|---|---|---|
| Fifth Plan 1974–9 | 1,027.00 | 403.07 | 39.25 |
| Annual Plan 1979–80 | 260.00 | 94.71 | 36.43 |
| Sixth Plan 1980–5 | 1,957.00 | 732.94 | 37.45 |
| Seventh Plan 1985–90 | 3,285.00 | 1,638.00 | 49.89 |
| Annual Plan 1990–1 | 905.00 | 350.00 | 38.69 |
| Annual Plan 1991–2 | 1,010.00 | 350.00 | 34.65 |
| Eighth Plan 1992–7 | 6,570.00 | 2,417.50 | 36.80 |
| Annual Plan 1992–3 | 1,500.00 | 550.00 | 36.66 |
| Annual Plan 1993–4 | 1,250.00 | 496.61 | 39.73 |
| Annual Plan 1994–5 | 1,450.00 | 560.00 | 38.62 |
| Ninth Plan 1997–2002 | 11,500.00 | 2,927.27 | 25.45 |

*Sources*: 1. Eighth Five Year Plan Document.
2. Planning Commission, April 2000, pp. 14–15.

period 1974–5 to 1998–9 is presented in Table 2.2 The total installed capacity from both hydro and thermal power plants was 878.38 MW on 31 March 1975, which rose to 3,964 MW by 31 March 1999. The compound growth rate of the installed generating capacity during this period comes out to be 6.48 per cent. The generating capacity of hydro power grew at the rate of 4.08 per cent while the generating capacity of thermal power grew at a much faster rate of 12.91 per cent during the same period. Of the total hydro power-generation capacity allocated to Punjab, the PSEB owned only a small hydro power-generating capacity, which amounted to 546.45 MW and a share of 1,297.6 MW in the Bhakra–Nangal Complex (BNC) and the Beas projects which have a total generating capacity of 2,793.65 MW. The Bhakra–Beas Management Board (BBMB), which controls the BNC and the Beas projects, is a central autonomous body. Punjab also has a share of 1,080 MW in the other central hydro, thermal, and gas-based power projects. One more hydro power plant of 600 MW capacity, at the Ranjit Sagar Dam, has been commissioned. The detailed composition of installed capacity as on 31 March 1999 is presented in Annexure 2.1. Though the increase in the generating capacity has been quite impressive, it has not been adequate to meet the increasing demand.

Total power generation by the Punjab Electric Power System was 1,798.68 million units (MUs) in 1974–5 which increased to 19,862.68 MUs in 1998–9 (Table 2.3). This shows that the electricity generated by the PSEB during this period of 24 years has increased at a phenomenal compound growth rate of 10.49 per cent. The highest growth rate of 19.94 per cent during the period was recorded by thermal power, followed by PSEB owned hydro plants (8.61 per cent), and the share from the common pool power generation (from the BBMB) grew at a rate of 7.06 per cent per annum.

Besides the two previously established thermal plants in Punjab, namely the Guru Gobind Singh Thermal Plant (GGSTP), Ropar and the Guru Nanak Dev Thermal Plant (GNDTP), Bhatinda, a new thermal plant, the Guru Hargobind Thermal Plant of 420 MW capacity, was commissioned in 1998–9. During the year of commissioning the new plant was in the process of stabilization. Therefore, its performance has not been evaluated. Table 2.4 shows the performance of the two older thermal plants in terms of the plant load factor (PLF) for the period 1985–6 to 1998–9. The performance of

TABLE 2.2: INSTALLED CAPACITY 1974–5 TO 1998–9

*(in MW)*

| S. No. | Description | Installed Capacity as on | | | | | |
|---|---|---|---|---|---|---|---|
| | | 31.3.1975 | 31.3.1980 | 31.3.1985 | 31.3.1990 | 31.3.1995 | 31.3.1999 |
| A | Hydro Power Houses | | | | | | |
| A.1 | Punjab's Share From Common Pool Projects | | | | | | |
| (i) | Pb's share from BNC | 613.000 | 613.120 | 689.414 | 689.414 | 689.414 | 731.304 |
| (ii) | Pb's share from Dehar P.H. | — | 316.800 | 475.200 | 475.200 | 475.200 | 475.200 |
| (iii) | Pb's share from Pong P.H. | — | 59.760 | 89.640 | 89.640 | 89.640 | 91.130 |
| | Total (A.1) | 613.000 | 989.680 | 1254.254 | 1254.254 | 1254.254 | 1297.638 |
| | Compound Growth Rate (A.1) (1975 to 1999) | | | | | | 3.17 |
| A.2 | Own Power Houses | | | | | | |
| (i) | Shanan P.H. | 48.486 | 48.486 | 60.486 | 60.000 | 60.000 | 60.000 |
| (ii) | Shanan Extention | — | — | 50.000 | 50.000 | 50.000 | 50.000 |
| (iii) | UBDC P.H.-I | 45.000 | 45.000 | 45.000 | 45.000 | 45.000 | 45.000 |
| (iv) | UBDC P.H.-II | — | — | — | 15.450 | 46.350 | 46.350 |
| (v) | Mukerian Hydro P.H. | — | — | 45.000 | 207.000 | 207.000 | 207.000 |
| (vi) | Anandpur Sahib Hydro P.H. | — | — | — | 134.000 | 134.000 | 134.000 |
| (vii) | Nidampur Micro Hydel P.H. | — | — | — | 1.000 | 1.000 | 1.000 |
| (viii) | Daudhar Micro Hydel P.H. | — | — | — | 1.500 | 1.500 | 1.500 |
| (ix) | Thuhi Micro Hydel P.H. | — | — | — | 0.800 | 0.800 | 0.800 |
| (x) | Rohti Micro Hydel P.H. | — | — | — | 0.800 | 0.800 | 0.800 |

| | | | | | | | |
|---|---|---|---|---|---|---|---|
| | Total (A.2) | 93.486 | 93.486 | 200.486 | 515.55 | 546.45 | 546.45 |
| | Compound Growth Rate (A.2) (1975 to 1999) | | | | | | 7.63 |
| | Total (A) | 706.486 | 1,083.166 | 1,451.74 | 1,769.804 | 1,800.704 | 1,844 |
| | Compound Growth Rate (2) (1975 to 1999) | | | | | | 4.08 |
| B | Thermal Power Houses | | | | | | |
| (i) | Nangal Thermal P.H. | 5 | — | — | Disp. Off | — | |
| (ii) | GNDTP Bhatinda | 110 | 440 | 440 | 440 | 440 | 440 |
| (iii) | GGSTP (Stage–I) Ropar | — | — | 420 | 420 | 420 | 420 |
| (iv) | GGSTP (Stage–II) Ropar | — | — | — | 420 | 420 | 420 |
| (v) | GGSTP (Stage–III) Ropar | — | — | — | — | 420 | 420 |
| (vi) | GHTP Lehra Mohabbat | — | — | — | — | — | 420 |
| | Total (B) | 115 | 440 | 860 | 1,280 | 1,700 | 2,120 |
| | Compound Growth Rate (1975 to 1999) | | | | | | 12.90 |
| C | RSTP Jalkheri | — | — | — | — | 10 | |
| D | Diesel Power House | 56.90 | 14.08 | 10.56 | — | — | |
| | Grand Total (A+B+C+D) | 878.386 | 1,537.246 | 2,325.3 | 3,049.804 | 3,510.704 | 3,964 |
| | Compound Growth Rate (A+B+C+D) (1974–5 to 1998–9) | | | | | | 6.48 |

*Source*: PSEB, *Annual Administration Reports*, various years.

TABLE 2.3: GROSS GENERATION OF ELECTRICITY 1974–5 TO 1998–9

*(in million units)*

| Year | Thermal Power Project | Hydro Power Project | Common Pool Power Projects | Gross Generation |
|---|---|---|---|---|
| | 1 | 2 | 3 | 4 (1+2+3) |
| 1974–5 | 151.93 | 482.74 | 1,164.01 | 1,798.68 |
| 1979–80 | 1,140.94 | 485.36 | 3,630.34 | 5,256.64 |
| 1984–5 | 2,938.27 | 966.00 | 3,592.80 | 7,497.07 |
| 1989–90 | 6,514.14 | 2,664.44 | 4,097.19 | 13,275.77 |
| 1994–5 | 8,439.14 | 3,068.66 | 4,555.66 | 16,063.46 |
| 1998–9 | 10,913.79 | 3,504.97 | 5,309.01 | 19,727.77 |
| Compound Growth Rate | 19.94 | 8.61 | 6.53 | 10.49 |

*Sources*: PSEB, *Energy Statistics of Punjab as on 31.3.1995* and *Annual Statement of Accounts 1998–99.*

thermal power plants in Punjab has been better than the all-India average. However, it has been reported by the officials of the board that the inadequate availability of coal of the appropriate quality, shortage of maintenance equipment, equipment failures, etc., are some of the major factors which have acted as constraints to the improvement in the performance of Punjab's thermal power plants. If these deficiencies, can be overcome, there is no reason why these thermal power plants cannot achieve a performance comparable to the NTPC plants.

Demand-side factors can be analysed in terms of the growth and composition of energy consumption, the connected load, and the number of consumers. Table 2.5 presents the consumer category-wise annual sale of energy during the period 1974–5 to 1998–9. The total sale of energy increased from 1,562.50 MUs in 1974–5 to 21,004.11 MUs in 1998–9 at a compound growth rate of 11.43 per cent. The energy consumed by large industries showed a spectacular increase at the rate of 13.67 per cent during the period, which was followed by domestic consumers (13.51 per cent), medium industries (11.99 per cent), and agricultural consumers (10.43 per cent). The share of domestic consumption increased from about 11 per cent in 1974–5 to 17 per cent in 1998–9. The share of commercial consumers remains

TABLE 2.4: PERFORMANCE OF THERMAL POWER PLANTS 1985–6 TO 1998–9 (PLANT LOAD FACTORS)

(*per cent*)

| | Capacity (MW) | 1985–6 | 1988–9 | 1991–2 | 1994–5 | 1996–7 | 1997–8 | 1998–9 |
|---|---|---|---|---|---|---|---|---|
| Guru Nanak Dev Thermal Plant, Bhatinda | 440 | 60.5 | 58.8 | 49.5 | 63.2 | 67.5 | 65.1 | 66.7 |
| Guru Gobind Singh Thermal Plant, Ropar | 1,260 | 58.9 | 45.9 | 54.5 | 54.4 | 65.0 | 70.3 | 70.0 |
| PSEB | 1,700 | 58.9 | 56.1 | 52.8 | 56.7 | 65.0 | 69.1 | 69.2 |
| All India | — | 52.4 | 55.0 | 55.3 | 60.0 | 64.4 | 64.7 | 64.6 |

*Sources*: 1. Planning Commission April 2000.
2. PSEB, *Annual Statements of Accounts*, various issues.

TABLE 2.5: CATEGORY-WISE SALE OF ENERGY 1974–5 TO 1998–9

*(in million units)*

| Category | 1974–5 | 1979–80 | 1984–5 | 1990–1 | 1994–5 | 1998–9 | Compound Growth Rate |
|---|---|---|---|---|---|---|---|
| 1. Domestic | 171.72 | 386.86 | 654.03 | 1,521.82 | 2383.32 | 3,595.69 | 13.51 |
| | (10.99) | (9.47) | (11.14) | (13.04) | (16.04) | (17.12) | |
| 2. Commercial | 70.15 | 110.36 | 134.20 | 294.68 | 459.98 | 785.11 | 10.59 |
| | (4.49) | (2.70) | (2.29) | (2.52) | (3.10) | (3.74) | |
| 3. Small Power | 143.35 | 257.36 | 297.17 | 483.56 | 608.86 | 675.54 | 6.67 |
| | (9.17) | (6.30) | (5.06) | (4.14) | (4.10) | (3.22) | |
| 4. Medium Power | 91.62 | 252.33 | 386.30 | 637.42 | 796.93 | 1,170.59 | 11.99 |
| | (5.86) | (6.18) | (6.58) | (5.46) | (5.36) | (5.57) | |
| 5. Large Power | 246.64 | 911.22 | 1,656.25 | 3,115.90 | 4,302.51 | 5,341.45 | 13.67 |
| | (15.78) | (22.30) | (28.22) | (26.69) | (28.96) | (25.43) | |
| 6. Agricultural | 695.66 | 1,896.21 | 2,358.99 | 5,095.31 | 5,979.76 | 7,531.99 | 10.43 |
| | (44.52) | (46.41) | (40.19) | (43.65) | (40.25) | (35.86) | |
| 7. Bulk Supply | 137.88 | 260.84 | 365.95 | 500.86 | 290.50 | 350.07 | 3.96 |
| | (8.82) | (6.38) | (6.23) | (4.29) | (1.96) | (1.66) | |
| 8. Street Lighting | 5.48 | 10.23 | 16.63 | 23.00 | 33.24 | 53.59 | 9.97 |
| | (0.35) | (0.25) | (0.28) | (0.20) | (0.22) | (0.26) | |
| Total | 1,562.50 | 4,085.41 | 5,869.52 | 11,672.55 | 14,855.10 | 21,004.11 | 11.43 |

*Note*: Figures in parentheses show percentages.
*Sources*: PSEB, *Energy Statistics of Punjab as on 31.3.1995*, and *Annual Statement of Accounts 1998–99*.

around 3 to 4 per cent. The share of large industrial consumers increased from about 16 per cent to 26 per cent during this period. The share of total energy consumed by the industrial consumers increased from 31 to 38 per cent during the period. The share of agricultural consumers was estimated around 45 per cent in 1974–5, and then it declined to 35.86 per cent by 1998–9. Thus, industry and agriculture continued to be the most important categories of consumers in terms of their relative shares. An analysis of the relative shares in the consumption of various categories of consumers requires extra caution, as the estimates of electric energy consumed by the agricultural sector are at best intelligent guesses.

The consumer category-wise connected load during the period 1974–5 to 1998–9 is given in Table 2.6. The total connected load increased from about 1,684 MW in 1974–5 to 12,459 MW in 1998–9, showing a compound growth rate of 8.70 per cent. A category-wise analysis of the connected load shows that the domestic sector achieved the highest growth rate of 11.11 per cent, followed by the large power sector (10.60 per cent). The commercial load grew at a rate of 9.28 per cent and the small power category showed a relatively lower growth rate of 5.19 per cent during the period. The agricultural connected load was quite high. Table 2.7 presents the category-wise details of the number of consumers of electricity in Punjab from 1974–5 to 1998–9. The total number of consumers, which stood at 1,176,420 in 1974–5, increased to 4,919,450 by the end of 1994–5, showing a compound growth rate of 6.24 per cent. Industry and agricultural consumers registered growth rates of more than 7 per cent.

The above analysis of the expansion in generation capacity and energy generation as well as of demand expansion in terms of energy consumption, connected load, and number of consumers clearly establishes that the system has registered quite an impressive increase. The per capita consumption of electricity in Punjab is about 840 units as compared to the all-India average of about 340 units.[2] In fact, electricity has made a significant contribution to the growth of the Punjab economy as well as in raising the standard of living of the people in the state.

The 15th Power Survey Committee constituted by the Central Electricity Authority (CEA) made a forecast of Punjab's power position up to the end of the Ninth Five Year Plan (Table 2.8). It estimated that the energy shortage will remain in the range of 11 to 17 per cent and that the peaking capacity shortage will be of the order of 25 to 30 per

TABLE 2.6: CATEGOR-WISE CONNECTED LOAD 1974–5 TO 1998–9

(*in KW*)

| Category | 1974–5 | 1979–80 | 1984–5 | 1989–90 | 1994–5 | 1998–9 | Compound Growth Rate |
|---|---|---|---|---|---|---|---|
| 1. Domestic | 347,513 | 705,301 | 1,177,365 | 1,806,916 | 3,068,901 | 4,379,359 | 11.11 |
| 2. Commercial | 118,796 | 204,577 | 293,912 | 446,496 | 662,493 | 999,838 | 9.28 |
| 3. Small Power | 254,645 | 364,627 | 476,838 | 662,459 | 782,392 | 851,401 | 5.19 |
| 4. Medium Power | 116,250 | 232,728 | 341,210 | 538,419 | 720,438 | 899,584 | 8.90 |
| 5. Large Power | 222,210 | 433,288 | 749,422 | 1,223,461 | 1,924,766 | 2,492,227 | 10.60 |
| 6. Agricultural | 592,824 | 961,308 | 1,405,850 | 1,910,324 | 2,423,584 | 2,679,829 | 6.49 |
| 7. Bulk Supply | 28,587 | 36,837 | 53,973 | 155,584 | 176,054 | 142,921 | 6.94 |
| 8. Street Lighting | 3,103 | 4,511 | 8,713 | 9,101 | 10,608 | 13,716 | 6.39 |
| Total | 1,683,928 | 2,943,177 | 4,507,283 | 6,752,760 | 9,769,236 | 12,458,875 | (100.00) |

*Source*: PSEB, *Annual Administration Report*, various issues.

TABLE 2.7: CATEGORY-WISE NUMBER OF CONSUMERS 1974–5 TO 1998–9

| Category | 1974–5 | 1979–80 | 1984–5 | 1989–90 | 1994–5 | 1998–9 | Compound Growth Rate |
|---|---|---|---|---|---|---|---|
| 1. Domestic | 839,103 | 1,374,506 | 1,989,507 | 2,600,914 | 2,999,710 | 3,485,829 | 6.11 |
| 2. Commercial | 163,756 | 221,432 | 286,505 | 372,226 | 434,114 | 560,190 | 5.26 |
| 3. Small Power | 30,770 | 43,733 | 60,168 | 81,502 | 86,420 | 89,354 | 4.54 |
| 4. Medium Power | 2,587 | 4,782 | 7,055 | 9,926 | 12,391 | 15,827 | 7.84 |
| 5. Large Power | 503 | 889 | 1,309 | 1,720 | 2,177 | 2,945 | 7.64 |
| 6. Agricultural | 139,151 | 254,330 | 410,519 | 565,092 | 703,374 | 759,649 | 7.33 |
| 7. Bulk Supply | 124 | 140 | 200 | 250 | 401 | 443 | 5.45 |
| 8. Street Lighting | 426 | 561 | 705 | 798 | 924 | 1,233 | 4.53 |
| Total | 1,176,420 | 1,900,373 | 2,755,968 | 3,632,428 | 4,239,511 | 4,919,450 | 6.24 |

*Source*: As in Table 2.6.

TABLE 2.8: PUNJAB'S PRESENT POWER POSITION AND FUTURE PROJECTION

(A) Power Supply Position on Energy Basis

*(MUs)*

| Year | Requirement | Availability | Deficit | Percentage |
|---|---|---|---|---|
| 1994–5 | 21,151 | 19,260 | –1,891 | –8.94 |
| 1995–6 | 22,465 | 19,672 | –2,793 | –12.43 |
| 1996–7 | 23,988 | 19,735 | –4,253 | –17.73 |
| 1997–8 | 25,439 | 21,377 | –4,062 | –15.97 |
| 1998–9 | 26,937 | 23,319 | –3,618 | –13.43 |
| 1999–2000 | 28,551 | 24,998 | –3,553 | –12.44 |
| 2000–1 | 30,233 | 26,763 | –3,470 | –11.48 |
| 2001–2 | 31,997 | 30,664 | –1,333 | –4.17 |

(B) Power Supply Position on Peak Demand Basis

*(MW)*

| Year | Requirement | Availability | Deficit | Percentage |
|---|---|---|---|---|
| 1994–5 | 3,950 | 2,945 | –1,005 | –25.44 |
| 1995–6 | 4,179 | 3,004 | –1,175 | –28.12 |
| 1996–7 | 4,445 | 3,024 | –1,421 | –31.97 |
| 1997–8 | 4,695 | 3,162 | –1,533 | –32.65 |
| 1998–9 | 4,952 | 3,589 | –1,363 | –27.52 |
| 1999–2000 | 5,228 | 3,908 | –1,320 | –25.25 |
| 2000–1 | 5,515 | 4,202 | –1,313 | –23.81 |
| 2001–2 | 5,814 | 4,653 | –1,161 | –19.47 |

*Source*: Central Electricity Authority, 15th Power Survey Committee (GOI) Year 1995.

cent.[3] Extra efforts are needed to rectify this situation. Otherwise, the pace of economic development in the state will be hampered.

## 2. FINANCIAL POSITION OF THE PSEB

The financial management of the SEBs in India is governed by section 59 of the Electricity (Supply) Act, 1948. Its latest provisions are:

1. The Board shall after taking credit for any subvention from the state government under section 63, carry on its operations under this Act and adjust its tariff so as to ensure that the total revenue in any year of account shall, after meeting all expenses properly chargeable to revenues including operating, maintenance and

management expenses, taxes (if any) on income and profits, depreciation and interest payable on all debentures, bonds and loans, leave such surplus as is not less than 3 per cent or such higher percentage as the state government may, by notification in the official Gazette, specify in this behalf, of the value of the fixed assets of the Board in service at the beginning of such year.

2. In specifying any higher percentage under sub-section (1), the state government shall have due regard to the availability of the amount accrued by way of depreciation and the liability for loan amortization and leave (a) a reasonable sum to contribute towards the cost of capital works; and (b) wherein respect of the Board, a notification has been issued under sub-section (1) of section 12A, a reasonable sum by way of return on capital provided by the state government under sub-section (3) of the section and the amount of the loan (if any) converted by the state government into capital under sub-section (1) of section 66A.

As the Government of India was not satisfied with the financial performance of the SEBs, it made a 3 per cent rate of return (ROR) on the average capital base an obligatory ROR for the SEBs by amending section 59 of the Act w.e.f. 1 April 1985.[4]

It will be useful to quickly review the recommendations of various expert committees in relation to the financial management and performance of the SEBs. The financial position of the electricity undertakings was examined for the first time by a working group constituted by the Planning Commission (ISI Group) in 1962.[5] In this report, the average cost pricing method based on the cost of service was advocated. The Committee recommended that the SEBs should earn a return of 12 per cent (including electricity duty) on capital investment after providing for operating expenses and depreciation. The capital base was to be calculated on the basis of the definition given in the Electricity (Supply) Act, 1948. The working group found that the average ROR for the country as a whole in 1957–8 was 3.9 per cent. The comparison of cost of service to various consumer classes and average revenue realized showed that large industries and agricultural consumers were being highly subsidized, domestic consumption and public lighting were being charged at par, and the commercial and shall industrial consumers were being charged at more than the cost of service. Thus, there was a lot of cross subsidization. It recommended a 32 per cent increase in price to achieve a 12 per cent ROR.

The Government of India was seriously concerned about the deteriorating financial position of the SEBs. It constituted a committee in 1964 under the chairmanship of R. Venkataraman to go into the financial position of the SEBs.[6] The committee examined the financial position of the SEBs in relation to the Electricity (Supply) Act, 1948. The main recommendations were as follows:

(a) The Boards should immediately achieve self-sufficiency, i.e. they should earn enough revenue to cover all the operational and maintenance costs, contributions to depreciation, and general reserve and interest on loans (paragraph 8).
(b) If the undertaking is running at a loss, it should move in two phases:
   (i) In the first phase (in the next three to five years), the Boards which do not earn enough to meet at least the cost of supply should begin to do so (paragraph 20).
   (ii) In the second phase (within three years of their achieving the first phase), the Board should fix their tariff in such a way that the gross revenue covers all the operational costs plus depreciation and leaves a return of 11 per cent on the investment made by the Board. The rationality of the 11 per cent rate of return was that the net profit of 3 per cent should be left on the average capital base. It was estimated that the average interest rate was 6 per cent, electricity duty 1.5 per cent, and general reserve 0.5 per cent. Thus, the 11 per cent gross return amounts to a ROR of 9.5 per cent excluding the state-imposed electricity duty, and a pure profit of 3 per cent which could be used for further investment (paragraph 23).
(c) Interest on investment on works in progress should be capitalized (paragraph 21).

It was recommended that as a general rule the board should supply power at a rate which meets at least the operations and maintenance cost, depreciation, and interest charges. The energy-intensive industries may be subsidized only after expert advice. The Committee estimated that for 1962–3, the ROR for various SEBs ranged from 0.7 per cent to 6.0 per cent. For Punjab (including Haryana), it was estimated to be 4.9 per cent.

The Energy Survey of India Committee, 1965, which carried out the first systematic survey of the energy requirements in the country broadly agreed with the ISI Group Study recommendations on electricity pricing.[7] A majority of the committee held the opinion that in the relatively risk-free public utilities in India, the ROR should not be less than 10 per cent. The Committee further suggested that in Indian conditions, 35 per cent to 40 per cent of the resources needed for further expansion should be generated from the internal resources of the utility. The report of the Sixth Finance Commission, 1973 which examined the finances of the SEBs during the Fourth Five Year Plan (1969–74) state:

> Despite all round awareness of the need to achieve a certain minimum rate of return on investment made in the power projects, the working results of the State Electricity Boards, far from registering any improvement, have suffered a set-back during the current Plan period. The forecasts furnished by the State Governments point to no significant improvement in the financial terms in the Fifth Five Year Plan period.[8]

The ROR on capital in the electricity sector for the country as a whole in 1969–70 was estimated to be 4.2 per cent, which declined to 3.3 per cent in 1973–4. The Finance Commission estimated the ROR of the HSEB to be 4.5 per cent, 4 per cent, and 3.2 per cent in the years 1971–2, 1972–3, and 1973–4 respectively.[9] The report of the Fuel Policy Committee, 1974 pointed out that many of the problems of the energy sector in India appeared to be due to the price policies of the fuel sector which had been concerned, possibly to a larger extent, with meeting one individual function of the policy, namely that of supplying consumers with energy at the lowest possible cost. As a result, the production of sufficient quantities of fuel had suffered and the country had also become increasingly dependent on external sources of supply.[10] The Committee pointed out that inadequate returns would adversely affect the power capacity expansion programmes and strongly recommended that the state must achieve the ROR suggested by the Venkataraman Committee. In fact, the Committee preferred a 10 per cent ROR (excluding electricity duty) in the case of electricity as it had done in the case of other sources of energy. The Committee recommended that while fixing tariff, a distinction should be made between peak and off-peak periods and that a penalty for use at the peak period should be attached to it. The Committee was against any type of subsidy in general. It argued strongly against the continuation of the subsidization of the agricultural sector, which could be justified as a promotional incentive at the initial stages of the energization of tube wells for irrigation. All the Five Year Plans as well as the Finance Commission

Reports emphasized that the electricity undertaking must generate internal resources to finance a part of the investment in the future.

The Committee on Power (1980), under the chairmanship of V.G. Rajadhyaksha, examined the financial position as well as the pricing policy of the SEBs in detail for the year 1977–8.[11] It was found that most of the SEBs could not achieve the 9.5 per cent ROR as recommended by the Venkataraman Committee. The average capital base has been defined as the average of the 'total capital at the beginning and end of the financial year'. The total capital is to be computed as follows:

(a) The gross value of fixed assets in operation plus (b) the cost of intangible assets plus (c) an amount on the account of working capital equal to one-sixth of administration and operating expenses (excluding provision for depreciation) for the fiscal year ending on the date under consideration reduced by (a) the amount of accumulated depreciation charged on the account of fixed assets in operation; and (c) the amount of security deposits of consumers.

The Committee estimated the ROR for 17 SEBs taken together for the year 1977–8 to be 7.9 per cent. It was estimated to be 6.5 per cent for Punjab. The Committee recommended that a 15 per cent ROR should be achieved on the average capital base as defined above. The idea behind the recommendation of a 15 per cent ROR, which was higher than the figure recommended by the Ventakaraman Committee (11 per cent), was based on the Rajadhyaksha Committee's estimate of the amount of resources required for investment over the period 1980 to 2000. It had recommended that electricity undertakings must generate internal resources to the extent of 50 per cent required for investment. To generate internal resources to this extent, a 15 per cent rate was estimated to be needed.[12] The Committee recommended that the tariff should be related to the cost of supply as well as to the consumer's capacity to pay.[13] The National Development Council (1995) set up a Committee on Power to examine, *inter alia*, measures to make the SEBs viable by recasting tariff, improving efficiency, and considering the delinking of distribution from generation. The Committee, known as the Sharad Pawar Committee on the State Electricity Boards, submitted its report to the National Development Council. It recommended that the SEBs should be restructured into corporate entities under the Companies Act.[14] It may be noted that a 3 per cent ROR is the minimum statutory requirement from the accounting year 1985. However, the SEBs have yet to comply with this statutory stipulation. Whereas in 1992–3 the number of SEBs with a positive ROR was seven, there were only three such SEBs in 1999–2000. Similarly, as against 12 SEBs with a negative ROR in 1992–3, the number of such SEBs has increased to 15 out of 19 in 1999–2000. There were only two relatively small SEBs with a ROR of more than 3 per cent in 1999–2000.[15] Thus the statutory provision of earning a 3 per cent ROR was violated both in letter and spirit by most of the SEBs, landing them into financial chaos.

It is obvious from a review of the various expert committee reports that recommendations have repeatedly emphasized that the SEBs must generate a surplus which is at least equal to the one recommended by the Venkataraman Committee. No consumer class may be subsidized without proper socio-economic considerations. Any provision for subsidy should be made explicit in the budget so that its justification may be determined.

In the light of the recommendations made by the various expert committees, the financial position of the PSEB has been analysed for the period 1995–6 to 1997–8. It may be noted from Table 2.9 that the average cost of supply increased from 60.45 paise per unit in 1985–6 to 205.86 paise per unit in 1998–9, representing an increase at the rate of 9.88 per cent per annum over the period under consideration. The average revenue realized from each category of consumers is a good proxy for the tariff rates. During the same period, the average revenue realized from commercial, industrial, and bulk supply consumers increased at rates higher than the cost of supply. In the 1990s, the average revenue realized from these categories of consumers was consistently higher than the average cost of supply. In the case of domestic consumers, the rate of growth of average revenue (9.37 per cent) was lower than the growth in the average cost of supply (9.88 per cent). The average revenue realized from domestic consumers was consistently lower than the cost of supply, implying the subsidization of the domestic supply. The average revenue realized from agricultural consumers increased from 16.52 paise per unit in 1985–6 to 28.46 paise per unit in 1996–7, and thereafter, in 1997–8, electricity supply to agriculture was made free of cost. In the 1990s, the gap between the average revenue realized per unit of electricity sale and the average cost of supply has consistently widened. The

TABLE 2.9: AVERAGE REVENUE REALIZED EXCLUDING ELECTRICITY DUTY AND AVERAGE COST OF SUPPLY 1985–6 TO 1998–9

*(Paise per unit)*

| | 1985–6 | 1988–9 | 1991–2 | 1994–5 | 1996–7 | 1999–8 | 1998–9 | Growth Rate |
|---|---|---|---|---|---|---|---|---|
| Domestic | 58.92 | 70.50 | 86.05 | 120.33 | 144.88 | 159.72 | 188.75 | 9.37 |
| Commercial | 91.60 | 96.72 | 148.97 | 200.30 | 261.64 | 287.28 | 331.23 | 10.39 |
| Small Power | 57.79 | 67.74 | 92.40 | 148.30 | 208.30 | 214.32 | 244.08 | 11.72 |
| Medium Powe | 53.15 | 65.76 | 108.44 | 167.93 | 231.41 | 227.28 | 245.60 | 12.49 |
| Large Supply | 49.32 | 61.40 | 97.45 | 166.96 | 233.70 | 264 | 292.58 | 14.68 |
| Agricultural | 16.52 | 8.48 | 9.71 | 34.49 | 28.46 | — | — | — |
| Public Lighting | 81.37 | 87.32 | 110.26 | 161.30 | 283.89 | 232.96 | 357.14 | 12.05 |
| Bulk & Grid Supply | 43.81 | 58.67 | 98.17 | 146.64 | 223.84 | 240.23 | 287.73 | 15.58 |
| Common Pool Supply | 22.38 | 21.49 | 116.70 | 160.60 | 353.92 | 421.96 | 539.90 | 27.74 |
| Average Revenue | 52.27 | 60.85 | 94.64 | 143.87 | 153.69 | 164.31 | 169.79 | 9.48 |
| Average Cost of Supply | 60.45 | 98.40 | 98.77 | 152.37 | 167.07 | 193.83 | 205.86 | 9.88 |
| Net per Unit Gain/Loss on Sale | –8.18 | –37.55 | –4.13 | –8.50 | –13.38 | –29.52 | –36.07 | — |

*Source*: PSEB, Annual Statement of Accounts, various issues.

impact of the pricing policy on the financial health of the PSEB is presented in Table 2.10 The ROR on average capital base (Col. 4) has been consistently negative or low. The effective subsidy to agriculture has increased over time and was very high (Rs. 1,557 crore in 1999–2000). The subsidy to domestic consumption has also increased over time and stood at Rs. 280 crore in 1999–2000. Commercial losses increased to Rs. 1,223 crore. Such a financial position proved to be unsustainable over the long run. The provision of free supply of electricity has been done to appease the politically and economically dominant agricultural class of rich peasants and landlords. It has been established beyond doubt that the major part of the electricity subsidy to agricultural consumers is cornered by the big landlords and the rich peasants in the name of the *kisan*.[16] At the present stage of agricultural development in Punjab, there is little justification for the free supply of electricity except to certain marginal farmers who could be subsidized on socio-economic grounds. Moreover, in case subsidization is required to be undertaken on welfare or populist grounds, then the state government must financially compensate the PSEB.

The financial performance of the PSEB is quite unsatisfactory and

TABLE 2.10: EXTENT OF SUBSIDY 1990–1 TO 1998–9

(*Rs. in crore*)

| Year | Effective Subsidy for Agricultural Consumers | Subsidy for Domestic Consumers | Total (3=1+2) | ROR on Average Capital Base | Commercial Losses with Subsidy |
|---|---|---|---|---|---|
| | 1 | 2 | 3 | 4 | 5 |
| 1990–1 | 499.66 | 47.48 | 547.14 | –23.90% | 580.00 |
| 1991–2 | 498.91 | 20.34 | 519.25 | –15.73% | 410.00 |
| 1992–3 | 687.00 | 54.30 | 741.30 | –19.90% | 626.00 |
| 1993–4 | 797.00 | 83.10 | 977.76 | –20.90% | 693.00 |
| 1994–5 | 781.00 | 108.10 | 889.10 | –19.40% | 681.00 |
| 1995–6 | 829.00 | 119.60 | 948.60 | –21.10% | 644.00 |
| 1996–7 | 999.00 | 156.60 | 1,155.60 | –18.27% | 606.00 |
| 1997–8 | 1,326.00 | 237.80 | 1,563.80 | –33.21% | 979.00 |
| 1998–9 | 1,541.00 | 291.40 | 1,832.40 | –46.76% | 1,381.00 |
| 1999–2000 | 1,557.00 | 280.00 | 1,837.00 | –29.93% | 1,223.00 |

*Sources*: Planning Commission, 1994 and 2000.

the board incurred a commercial loss of Rs. 1,381 crore in 1998–9. This loss is partly due to the policy of the government to supply electricity free of cost to the agricultural consumers and at a subsidized rate to the domestic consumers. Unless the financial health of the board is improved, it may not be possible to generate internal resources for making additions to the generating capacity.

## 3. TRANSMISSION AND DISTRIBUTION LOSSES IN PUNJAB

The power system comprises generation, transformation, transmission, and distribution systems. In the process of transmission, a part of the energy carried from the generating stations to the consumers through the transmission and distribution networks is lost on account of technical losses due to the inherent characteristics of the equipment, specifically 'resistance' to the flow of the electric current. The transformation of energy from one voltage to the other also involves the dissipation of some energy. But energy losses are also caused due to pilferage, defective meters, unmetered supply, etc. The total losses on account of both the above-stated categories constitute the computed transmission and distribution (T&D) losses or system losses.

T&D losses are an inseparable component of any power transmission and distribution network, and take place at various stages of the system right from the generating station down to the consumer. In view of the present shortage of power in the state and the poor financial performance of the PSEB, it becomes all the more important to reduce the T&D losses to the minimum level possible.

Various expert committees have recommended that high priority should be given to the reduction in line losses and that it should be ensured that line losses are steadily brought down. The Central Electricity Authority (CEA) has recommended 15 per cent T&D technical energy losses (4 per cent as transmission losses and 11 per cent as distribution losses) as the maximum norm at the present quality of the transmission and distribution network.[17]

### *Computation of T&D Losses and Official Estimates*

The PSEB keeps a quantity account of the electric energy generated and sold by metering the supply at various ends. Metering covers energy generated at the generating stations and the energy sold to consumers other than agricultural consumers to whom energy was supplied at a flat rate up to 1997–8, and thereafter it is being suppiied free. Supply to agriculture is not metered. Energy received and sold (feeder wise) through the sub-transmission and distribution system is expected to be metered by the Board for energy audit, but this information is not utilized for the computation of system losses. Since there is no way to assess the T&D losses separately, the Board has been computing the overall system losses merely as the difference between the total power available for sale and the power sold within and outside the state. The total system losses as computed by the Board from 1974–5 to 1999–2000 are given in Table 2.11

Table 2.11 shows that T&D losses, which were 24.03 per cent in 1974–5, were brought down to 17.7 per cent in 1999–2000. About 40 per cent of the total electricity supply in the state, including the agricultural sector, is unmetered and consumption is an estimate, which conceals more than what it actually reveals. It was reported that pilferage of power was being shown as a part of agricultural con-

TABLE 2.11: T&D LOSSES 1974–5 TO 1999–2000

| Year | Net Energy Available for Sale in Punjab (Excluding Common Pool) | Unaccounted Energy | T&D Losses (%) |
|---|---|---|---|
| | 1 | 2 | 3=2 × 100/1 |
| 1974–5 | 2,051.95 | 493.15 | 24.03 |
| 1979–80 | 5,290.26 | 1,207.25 | 22.82 |
| 1984–5 | 7,536.53 | 1,434.19 | 19.03 |
| 1989–90 | 15,025.13 | 2,838.39 | 18.96 |
| 1990–1 | 15,380.80 | 2,945.34 | 19.00 |
| 1991–2 | 16,168.94 | 3,033.36 | 18.76 |
| 1992–3 | 17,573.59 | 3,285.73 | 18.70 |
| 1993–4 | 18,652.88 | 3,443.93 | 18.46 |
| 1994–5 | 19,427.95 | 3,558.70 | 18.32 |
| 1995–6 | 20,065.90 | 3,652 | 18.20 |
| 1996–7 | 22,153.40 | 4,187 | 18.90 |
| 1997–8 | 22,859.60 | 4,069 | 17.80 |
| 1998–9 | 25,070.20 | 4,287 | 17.10 |
| 1999–2000 | 26,045.20 | 4,610 | 17.70 |

*Sources*: Planning Commission, 1994 and 2000.

sumption and T&D losses shown for a particular year were more of a policy decision than a true estimate. However, even these official estimates are still higher than the Central Electricity Authority (CEA) norm of 15 per cent, which warrants the adoption of steps to reduce them.

The report of the Comptroller and Auditor General for the year ended 31 March 1992 makes very revealing observations:[18]

1. The PSEB has reported that T&D losses during the period 1986–7 to 1990–1 were in the range of 18.19 per cent to 19.00 per cent. These are under-estimates. The report estimates that the actual T&D losses would be in the range of 29.70 per cent to 34.03 per cent.
2. Assuming the T&D losses to be 15 per cent as per the CEA recommended norms, during 1986–91 the loss of revenue to the PSEB was estimated to be Rs. 499.38 crore and the loss of electricity duty to the state government was estimated to be to the tune of Rs. 44.38 crore.
3. These excessive losses were equivalent to 502 MW of power, the generation, transmission, and distribution of which required capital investment of the order of Rs. 1,707 crore. Thus, the report clearly brings out the gravity of the problem of the pilferage of power in the state of Punjab.

The main reason for the high T&D losses as against the norm of 15 per cent recommended by the CEA are as follows:

1. *Inadequate transmission system*: The completion of transmission lines and sub-stations simultaneously with the commissioning of the generating capacity is of vital importance for the evacuation of power. Moreover, the transmission system must keep pace with the increase in the generating capacity to avoid overloading, ensure proper voltage, and improve the reliability of the system as a whole.

2. *Imbalance of investment in the transmission system*: The Rajadhyaksha Committee on Power (1980) had recommended that investment in the generation system must be accompanied by a matching investment in the transmission and distribution systems and that the expenditure on generation, transmission, distribution, and rural electrification should be in the ratio of 4:2:1:1. It was found that during the five-year period from 1986–7 to 1990–1, against an investment of Rs. 1,609.74 crore in generation, the investment in transmission amounted to Rs. 249.98 crore. The investment in generation and

transmission was thus in the ratio of 4:0.62 as against the recommended ratio of 4:2.

## 4. EXTENT OF POWER THEFT IN PUNJAB AND REMEDIAL MEASURES TAKEN BY THE PSEB

Pilferge and theft of energy is one of the major contributory factors for the high quantum of T&D losses. As distrinct from technical losses which arise from certain inherent characteristics of the equipment and conductors used for transmitting and distributing power, the factors responsible for commercial losses can be broadly classified as follows:

(i) Inaccuracy in meters and metering equipment;
(ii) Defective meters/associated instrument transformers;
(iii) Meters/instrument transformers installed incommensurate with the actual load;
(iv) Unaccounted supply of energy;
(v) Theft of energy by unscrupulous consumers either by passing/tampering with the meters or by using unauthorized extension of energy.

Theft/unauthorized extension of energy has become a big menance these days. The PSEB has set up flying squads under the control of the Director/Enforcement which carry out surprise checks/raids at the premises of consumers. The details of theft cases detected by the enforcement staff and the leakage of revenue plugged from 1983–4 to 1994–5 are given in Table 2.12. The extent of power theft given in the table shows only the tip of the iceberg. The actual number of theft cases, which often go unnoticed, may be much higher. Table 2.12 shows that a total number of 4,409 theft cases (including unauthorized extension and wrong metering) were detected by the enforcement staff and revenues of Rs. 149.3 lakh were realized. In 1994–5, the enforcement staff detected 5,518 such cases and the revenue realized from the guilty parties was Rs. 1,807.8 lakh. It has been reported that during 1997–8, 1998–9, and 1999–2000, the recovery for theft of power and malpractices in Punjab was Rs. 9.38 crore, Rs. 11.68 crore, and Rs. 15.89 crore respectively.[19]

In order to contain the theft of power, the PSEB has laid down remedial measures, which are described in the *Sales Manual* of the PSEB.[20]

TABLE 2.12: NUMBER OF THEFT CASES DETECTED BY ENFORCEMENT STAFF OF PSEB AND REVENUE REALIZED 1983–4 TO 1994–5

| Year | Total No. of Connections (in thousands) | No. of Connections Checked/Raids | No. of Theft Cases Detected | No. of Unauthorized Ext. Cases Detected | No. of Wrong Metering Detected | Misc. Cases Detected (Capacitors not in Operation, Seal Broken, etc.) | Total (i.e. Cols. (4+5+6+7) | Revenue Realized (Rs. in Lakhs) |
|---|---|---|---|---|---|---|---|---|
| 1 | 2 | 3 | 4 | 5 | 6 | 7 | 8 | 9 |
| 1983–4 | 2,732.54 | 11,223 | 695 | 1,196 | 1,502 | 1,016 | 4,409 | 149.30 |
| 1984–5 | 2,889.23 | 11,486 | 906 | 1,051 | 1,503 | 1,073 | 4,533 | 223.00 |
| 1985–6 | 3,060.67 | 18,080 | 2,819 | 1,290 | 2,129 | 2,176 | 8,414 | 227.90 |
| 1986–7 | 3,114.29 | 18,770 | 1,486 | 1,123 | 1,971 | 3,249 | 7,829 | 531.90 |
| 1987–8 | 3,269.05 | 18,971 | 1,564 | 1,091 | 2,194 | 2,342 | 7,191 | 817.60 |
| 1988–9 | 3,441.89 | 15,710 | 1,146 | 1,961 | 2,157 | 1,369 | 6,633 | 869.10 |
| 1989–90 | 3,632.43 | 21,011 | 3,599 | 1,286 | 2,870 | 1,785 | 9,540 | 955.70 |
| 1990–1 | 3,749.77 | 20,375 | 1,546 | 1,750 | 2,653 | 965 | 6,914 | 1,115.80 |
| 1991–2 | 3,869.73 | 18,454 | 1,538 | 1,026 | 1,972 | 890 | 5,426 | 1,845.50 |
| 1992–3 | 3,989.52 | 20,380 | 2,009 | 932 | 2,308 | 975 | 6,224 | 1,087.10 |
| 1993–4 | 4,184.84 | 19,114 | 2,177 | 1,032 | 2,048 | 813 | 6,070 | 1,883.70 |
| 1994–5 | 4,239.51 | 17,151 | 2,031 | 903 | 1,867 | 717 | 5,518 | 1,807.80 |

*Source*: Directorate of Enforcement, PSEB, Patiala. It is reported that in 1997–8 and 1998–9, Rs. 9.38 crore and Rs. 11.68 crore respectively were recovered for power theft and malpractices in PSEB, Statement of Accounts, 1998–9.

These are:

1. The meter/metering equipment should be installed near the entrance, which is easily accessible for recording readings/checking connections.
2. The meter/metering equipment should be housed in metering boxes/ cubicles standardized by the Board.
3. The meter/metering equipment should be sealed by the field officials after ensuring the correctness of the connection.
4. The meter cupboard/meter terminal seals should be checked frequently, especially in the case of major consumers. The XEN(DS) should arrange surprise/secret recording of the MDI readings before the scheduled reading dates.
5. The cases of premises locked and of 'nil' consumption should be got investigated by the AE/AEE(DS).
6. Wherever a theft of energy is doubted in the premises of any consumer, the variation in consumption should be established by keeping the meter/metering equipment under observation after affixing paper seals. Variation registers should be maintained properly and meter inspectors should mention therein the cases of such consumers where there had been marked variations in consumption in a particular month, with respect to the normal consumption.
7. Proper control should be exercised on the work of meter inspectors, who should submit their reports to the AE/AEE(DS). The AE/ AEE(DS), who is responsible for compliance within 24 hours, should immediately attend to any points raised by the meter inspector. However, the meter inspectors should bring serious and suspicious cases to the notice of the XEN also.
8. In case of tube-well consumers, where the flat rate is applicable, intensive periodical checking should be carried out by the DS/ enforcement staff in each division. The enforcement staff should check the dimensions of motors as per the ISI standards and unauthorized extension and misuse of energy.
9. The cut-outs should be provided after the point of installation of the meter instead of before the installation of the meter. In other words, the service line should be connected directly to the meter and the cut-out should be provided on the lower side. The main board supporting the meter should be properly grouted and sealed.

10. No PT fuses should be provided on the secondary side of the supply to KWh/MDI meters. In the case of existing connections, arrangements should be made to remove the PT fuses immediately.
11. Any fuse provided by mistake on the secondary side of the CT circuit should be removed immediately.
12. The standard CT/PT metering unit should be provided in place of the old open type CT/PT.
13. There should be no joint in the CT/PT secondary connecting loads up to the meter.
14. The entry and exit holes for the cable in the CT/PT chamber should be plugged by putting in suitable sizes of cable glands.
15. Distribution transformers to be provided inside the consumers' premises should be of the indoor type having LT bushing inside the transformer's body. The LT bushing provided before the meters should be properly covered and sealed.
16. The meters with fake/tampered MEC seals of those having some other artificial means for the abstraction of energy should not be allowed.
17. The capacity of the metering CT should be of suitable capacity, matching with the sanctioned load/contract demand. The multiplying factor should be applied correctly. The entry pertaining to the capacity of the meter should be clearly made in the meter-reading record and ledger, preferably in red ink.
18. To prevent tampering/providing fake ME seals and to prevent tampering with the window glass and its fixing mechanism, the following are the remedies:
    - (i) The instructions regarding the affixing of paper seals must be rigidly followed by the officials/officers concerned;
    - (ii) Impression of ME seals may be stamped on the corners of the meter index plate with indelible ink.
    - (iii) ME seals should be of multifarious impressions and should be properly pressed by using the latest technique like hydraulic pressing, etc.

In addition to these measures the Board has laid down certain instructions to make the checking and the detection of theft of energy cases more effective.

### 1. *Maintenance of registers for checking and detecting theft of energy cases* (*Instruction No. 205*)

A register on the prescribed form 'Narrative Report on the Theft of Energy Cases' should be maintained in all sub-offices, sub-divisional offices for checking and detecting theft of energy cases wherein the details of theft of energy checked and investigated should be recorded. Each checking authority shall separately maintain this register.

2. *Responsibility of the field staff to check theft of energy* (*Instruction* No. 207)

The field officers/officials who are required to check and seal the meter equipment should take due care while affixing the seal to the meter/metering equipment. In case the seals affixed by them are found to be intact by the enforcement staff/checking authority, but the consumer is found to be indulging in theft of energy or if the meter is found to be recording less due to long connections, the situation shall be taken as the intentional connivance of such officers/officials and they will be held fully responsible for the consequences thereof. Suitable disciplinary action also be taken against the officers/officials/ concerned as per the rules. The following officials will be held responsible with respect to the specified category of connections:

| | |
|---|---|
| (a) All single phase connections and metered AP connections | Meter reader/meter inspector/ and lineman responsible for attending the complaint/ JE-I/JE-II |
| (b) 3 phase domestic/non-residential connections of board employees, street lighting, and SP connections | Meter readermeter inspector/ lineman responsible for attending the complaint/ JE-I/JE-II/AE/AEE(DS) |
| (c) Non-residential connections with CTs/PTs, bulk supply connections released on LT, all MS connections (with or without CTs/PTs), and MDIs of all LS consumers. | Meter inspector/JE-II/ JE-I/AE/AEE/XEN(DS) |

A review of the rules and procedures for the prevention of theft and pilferage of power prescribed by the board on the basis of the field survey conducted by the study team shows that these rules and procedures are not rigidly followed. They are generally flouted with the active connivance of the employees. The report of the Comptroller and Auditor General of India for the year ended 31 March 1992 in its review on 'T&D Losses of the PSEB' also found substantial shortfalls in the periodical checking of connections by the field staff. They also

TABLE 2.13: PERCENTAGE OF CONNECTIONS CHECKED BY FIELD STAFF AND ENFORCEMENT STAFF OF PSEB (1986–7 TO 1990–1)

| Year | Checking by Field Staff | | | Checking by Enforcement Staff | | |
|---|---|---|---|---|---|---|
| | No. of Connections | No. of Connections Checked | Percentage of Connections Checked | Total Connections (No. in Thousands) | No. of Connections Checked | Percentage of Connectoins Checked |
| 1986–7 | 2,367,764 | 318,780 | 13 | 3,114.29 | 19,770 | 0.63 |
| 1987–8 | 2,488,589 | 1,388,328 | 56 | 3,269.05 | 18,971 | 0.58 |
| 1988–9 | 2,626,771 | 1,449,434 | 55 | 3,441.89 | 15,710 | 0.46 |
| 1989–90 | 2,779,018 | 1,293,437 | 47 | 3,632.43 | 21,011 | 0.58 |
| 1990–1 | 2,852,719 | 1,176,100 | 41 | 3,749.77 | 20,375 | 0.54 |

*Source*: Report of the Comptroller and Auditor General of India for the year ended 31 March 1992, No. 1 (Commercial), Government of Punjab.

found that no norms had been prescribed for checking by the enforcement staff to detect cases of pilferage/theft of energy. Table 2.13 gives the percentage of connections checked by the field staff as well as the enforcement staff for the period 1986–7 to 1990–1.

Table 2.13 shows that the field staff was not checking the connections as per the prescribed norms. The percentage of connections checked was only 13 in 1986–7, which, however, increased to 41 in 1990–1. The board did not give the reasons for not checking the connections to the extent of the prescribed norms. Similarly, shortfalls were found in the checking by the enforcement staff, although the board had prescribed no norms. The percentage of connections checked came down from 0.63 in 1986–7 to 0.54 in 1990–1.

Thus, we can conclude that the theft of power is a serious problem in Punjab. It leads to a huge loss of revenue, which is desperately needed to restore the financial health of the PSEB. A strict compliance with the rules and procedures dealing with the prevention of theft of power is called for. Along with this, there is a need to devise ways and means to reduce the menace of power theft, which is the focus of attention in subsequent chapters.

## NOTES

1. Punjab State Electricity Board, *Annual Statement of Accounts,* and *Annual Administration Report for 1998–99*, Patiala.
2. Government of India, Ministry of Finance, *Economic Survey 2000–1*, New Delhi.
3. Government of India, Central Electricity Authority, *Fifteenth Annual Electric Power Survey of India*, New Delhi, 1996.
4. Government of India, *The Electricity (Supply) Act, 1948*, New Delhi, 1997.
5. Government of India, Planning Commission, *The Pricing of Electricity: Report of the Planning Unit of the Indian Statistical Institute (ISI)*, New Delhi, 1962.
6. Government of India, *Report of the Committee on the Working of the State Electricity Boards*, New Delhi, 1964.
7. Government of India, *Report of the Energy Survey of India Committee*, New Delhi, 1965.
8. Government of India, *Sixth Finance Commission Report*, New Delhi, 1973.
9. Ibid., p. 56.

10. Government of India, *Report of the Fuel Policy Committee*, New Delhi, 1974.
11. Government of India, Ministry of Energy, *Report of the Committee on Power*, New Delhi, 1980.
12. Ibid., p. 72.
13. Ibid., pp. 78–9.
14. Centre for the Monitoring of Indian Economy, *India's Energy Sector*, Bombay, 1995.
15. Government of India, Planning Commission, *Anual Report on the Working of State Electricity Boards and Electricity Departments*, New Delhi, 2000, p. 148.
16. Girish Sant and Shantanu Dixit, 'Beneficiaries of IPS Subsidy and Impact of Tariff Hikes', *Economic and Political Weekly*, vol. 31 no. 51, 21–8 December 1996.
17. (i) Electricity is transmitted at various voltage: 400 KV, 220 KV, 132 KV, 66 KV, and 33 KV. All the energy losses during transmission at these voltages are included in transmission losses. Electricity is generally distributed at 11 KV and 230 volts; energy lost in the process is known as distribution losses.

    (ii) Government of India, Ministry of Irrigation and Power, Power Economy Committee, *Report of the Study Group 11*, 1970.
18. Punjab State Electricity Board, *Report of the Comptroller and Auditor General for the year ended 31 March 1992*, 1995.
19. Punjab State Electricity Board, *Annual Statement of Accounts*, Schedule-2 for various years.
20. Punjab State Electricity Board, *Sales Manual*, Patiala, 1995.

## ANNEXURE 2.1: TOTAL INSTALLED CAPACITY AVAILABLE FOR PUNJAB AS ON 31 MARCH 1999

| Name of Project | Unit Capacity | Total Installed Capacity (MW) | PSEB Share | |
|---|---|---|---|---|
| | | | (MW) | Percentage |
| ***Own Hydro | | | | |
| Shanan Power House | (4 × 15 + 1 × 50 MW | 110.00 | 110.00 | 100.00 |
| UBDC–I | (3 × 15 MW) | 45.00 | 45.00 | 100.00 |
| Mukerian I & II | (6 × 15 + 6 × 19.5 MW) | 207.00 | 207.00 | 100.00 |
| A.S.H.P. | (4 × 33.5 MW) | 134.00 | 134.00 | 100.00 |
| UBDC-II | (3 × 15.45 MW) | 46.35 | 46.35 | 100.00 |
| Micro Hydel Schemes | (5 × 0.5 + 4 × 0.4 MW) | 4.10 | 4.10 | 100.00 |
| Sub Total | | 546.45 | 546.45 | 100.00 |
| ***Own Thermal | | | | |
| GNDTP Stage I & II | (4 × 110 MW) | 440.00 | 440.00 | 100.00 |
| GGSTP | (6 × 210 MW) | 1,260.00 | 1,260.00 | 100.00 |
| Rice Straw Jalkheri | (10 MW) | 10.00 | 10.00 | 100.00 |
| GGSTP Lahira Mahabat | (2 × 210 MW) | 420.00 | 420.00 | |
| Sub Total | | 2,130.00 | 2,130.00 | 100.00 |
| ***Common Pool | | | | |
| Bhakra Nangal Complex | (5 × 108 + 5 × 132 + 4 × 24.2 2 × 29.25 MW) | 1,355.30 | 689.41 | 50.87 |
| Dehar | (6 × 165 MW) | 990.00 | 475.20 | 48.00 |
| Pong | (6 × 60 MW) | 360.00 | 89.64 | 24.90 |
| Sub Total | | 2,705.30 | 1,254.25 | 46.36 |
| ***Central Thermal | | | | |
| Singrauli STPP | (5 × 200+2 × 500 MW) | 2,000.00 | 200.00 | 10.00 |
| Rihand-I STPP | (5 × 500 MW) | 1,000.00 | 110.00 | 11.00 |
| Unchahar-I TPS | (2 × 210 MW) | 420.00 | 36.00 | 8.57 |
| Sub Total | | 3,420.00 | 346.00 | 10.11 |
| ***Central Hydro | | | | |
| Bairasuil Hep | (3 × 66 MW) | 198.00 | 93.50 | 47.22 |
| Salal-I HEP | (3 × 115 MW) | 345.00 | 112.12 | 32.50 |
| Salal-II HEP | (2 × 115 MW) | 230.00 | 35.33 | 15.36 |
| Chamera-I HEP | (3 × 180 MW) | 540.00 | 82.90 | 15.35 |
| Sub Total | | 1,313.00 | 323.85 | 24.66 |

(Contd.)

ANNEXURE 2.1 (Contd.)

| Name of Project | Unit Capacity | Total Installed Capacity (MW) | PSEB Share | |
|---|---|---|---|---|
| | | | (MW) | Percentage |
| ***Central Gas | | | | |
| Anta CCGT | (3 × 88 + 1 × 149 MW) | 413.00 | 48.00 | 11.62 |
| Auriya CCGT | (4 × 112 + 2 × 102 MW) | 652.00 | 81.00 | 12.42 |
| Tanakpur HEP | (3 × 40 MW) | 120.00 | 18.00 | 15.00 |
| Dadri CCGT | (4 × 131 + 2 × 146.5 MW) | 817.00 | 130.00 | 15.91 |
| Sub Total | | 2,002.00 | 277.00 | 13.84 |
| ***Nuclear | | | | |
| Narora APP | (2 × 235 MW) | 470.00 | 55.00 | 11.70 |
| Sub Total | | 470.00 | 55.00 | 11.70 |
| Grand Total | | 12,166.75 | 4,512.55 | 37.09 |

*Source*: PSEB, Pataila.

CHAPTER 3

# Performance of the Haryana State Electricity Board

The main objective of this chapter is to evaluate the technical and financial performance of the erstwhile Haryana State Electricity Board (HSEB) since its inception in 1967 to 1998 when power reforms were introduced and the State Electricity Board was restructured and separate generation, transmission, and distribution companies were constituted under the Power Sector Reforms Act, 1997.

This chapter has been divided into five sections. Section 1 discusses the technical performance of the HSEB. Section 2 includes an analysis of the changing pattern of electricity consumption in the state. Section 3 examines the financial performance of the board. Section 4 is devoted to a discussion of the transmission and distribution losses. The section 5 reviews the experience of the power sector reforms in Haryana.

## 1. TECHNICAL PERFORMANCE OF THE HSEB

Haryana state came into existence with the reorganization of the former state of Punjab on 1 November 1966. Haryana consists of 19 districts covering a geographical area of 44,212 sq. km. Its total population at present is about two crore, inhabiting 6,759 villages and 81 towns and cities.[1] Haryana's economy is based on small peasant proprietorship. The HSEB was constituted by bifurcating the Punjab State Electricity Board (PSEB) in May 1967.

To meet the aspirations of the people of the newborn state, the state government initiated a massive programme of rapid economic development. Incidentally, this period coincides with the launching of Green Revolution, a strategy to bring about rapid agricultural development in India. This region was one of the major beneficiaries in terms of resource devolution from the central government. As infrastructure is of key importance in accelerating the process of economic development, it was realized that power should be made available at a reasonable price. The Plan expenditure incurred on the energy sector is presented in Table 3.1. Almost the entire expenditure on the energy sector was incurred on the electric power sector development in Haryana. It may be noted that expenditure on the energy sector ranged between 24.43 per cent and 38.39 per cent of the total Plan expenditure under various Five-Year Plans. In fact, the proportion of resources allocated to power was highest in the Fifth and Sixth Five Year Plans and next only to irrigation during the Fourth, Seventh, and Eighth Five Year Plans.

Haryana is acutely deficient in commercial energy resource endowment. It does not have coal or petroleum resources, and its hydropower potential is very small. Therefore, it depends heavily on its coal-based thermal power plants for which coal is transported over long distances. Haryana receives hydel power from interstate

TABLE 3.1: PLAN EXPENDITURE ON ENERGY SECTOR

*(Rs. in crores)*

| S. No. | Pariculars | Total Plan Expenditure | Expenditure on Energy | Energy Exp. as a Share of Total Exp. (4/3) (per cent) |
|---|---|---|---|---|
| 1 | 2 | 3 | 4 | 5 |
| 1. | Fourth Five Year Plan (1969–74) | 358.26 | 87.53 | 24.43 |
| 2. | Fifth Five Year Plan (1974–9) | 677.34 | 260.01 | 38.39 |
| 3. | Annual Plan (1979–80) | 202.95 | 56.40 | 27.79 |
| 4. | Sixth Five Year Plan (1980–5) | 15,995.47 | 491.62 | 30.81 |
| 5. | Seventh Five Year Plan (1985–90) | 2,510.64 | 639.03 | 25.45 |
| 6. | Annual Plan (1990–1) | 615.02 | 155.92 | 25.35 |
| 7. | Annual Plan (1991–2) | 699.39 | 182.97 | 36.16 |
| 8. | Eighth Five Year Plan (1992–7) | 4,889.89 | 1,197.68 | 24.49 |
| 9. | Ninth Five Year Plan (1997–2002) | 11,600.00 | 3,305.00 | 28.49 |

*Source*: *Statistical Abstract of Haryana*, various issues.

multipurpose hydro projects, namely the Bhakra Nangal projects and the Beas project which Haryana shares with other states. It also purchases power from various central and other state hydro and thermal power plants to meet additional demand for electricity.

The total installed generating capacity owned or shared by the HSEB as on 31 March 1998 was 2,392 MW (Table 3.2). The HSEB's own generating system consisted of two thermal power stations: 165 MW (3 × 55 MW) at Faridabad and 650 MW (4 × 110 MW + 1 × 210 MW) at Panipat. It also owned one micro hydel project of

TABLE 3.2: GENERATION CAPACITY AS ON 31 MARCH 1998

| S. No. | Name of the Power Station | Total Installed Capacity (MW) | Haryana's Share (MW) |
|---|---|---|---|
| A. | Hydro | | |
| | (i) Bhakra Nangal Complex | 1,405.30 | 477.00 |
| | (ii) Dehar Power House | 990.00 | 317.00 |
| | (iii) Pong Power House | 360.00 | 60.00 |
| | (iv) Central Hydro Project | 2,002.2 | 204.30 |
| | Total (A) | 4,757.50 | 1,058.30 |
| B. | Steam | | |
| | (i) Central Thermal Power Stations | 5,772.27 | 408.20 |
| | (ii) I.P. Station Ext. at Delhi | 187.50 | 62.50 |
| | Total (B) | 5,959.77 | 470.70 |
| C. | HSEB Own Projects | | |
| | (i) WYC Hydel Project (6 × 8 MW) | 48.00 | 48.00 |
| | (ii) Faridabad I Power Station 2 × 55 MW unit I & II 1 × 55 MW unit III | 165.00 | 165.00 |
| | (iii) Panipat Thermal Power Station 2 × 100 MW Stage I 2 × 110 MW Stage II 1 × 210 MW Stage III | 650.00 | 650.00 |
| | Total (C) | 863.00 | 863.00 |
| | Grand Total (A+B+C) | 11,580.27 | 2,392.00 |

*Source*: HSEB, *Annual Statement of Account*, 1997–98.

48 MW (6 × 8 MW) at the Western Yamuna Canal at Dadupur (Yamuna Nagar). Haryana is a partner in the Bhakra and Beas projects, which are controlled by the Bhakra Beas Management Board (BBMB). In the Bhakra system, its share was 477 MW and in the Beas system its share was 317 MW. Haryana has been allotted a share in the power-generating capacity in various central hydro and thermal projects in the northern region. Its share in the central hydel projects was 204.30 MW and in the central thermal projects, it was 408.20 MW. From the central projects, Haryana purchases electricity at tariff rates determined by respective central power corporations, which manage the power stations.

Table 3.3 summarizes the pace of growth in the generating capacity, energy generated, and other technical parameters during the period 1967–8 to 1997–8. It may be noted that the total installed capacity increased at 8.99 per cent per annum (from 383 MW to 1,173 MW) between 1967–8 and 1980–1. It grew at a relatively slow rate of 4.28 per cent from 1980–1 to 1997–8. The annual growth during the entire period comes out to be 6.29 per cent hydel-generating capacity expanded at a slower rate of 3.74 per cent in comparison to 15.99 per cent registered by the thermal-generating capacity. In fact, Haryana's own hydel power potential was very small and the increase in Haryana's share was contributed by the central government projects located in the adjoining states. During the period under review, the thermal power generation registered a growth rate of 18.25 per cent and hydel power a growth rate 5.71 per cent, making the overall growth rate in the electric energy generation 8.31 per cent per annum. An eleven-fold increase in the generation of electricity over a period of thirty years was quite a significant achievement.

During the period 1967–8 to 1997–8, simultaneous peak demand grew at a rate of 9.89 per cent per annum whereas energy sale increased at 9.76 per cent which was made possible by a 6.29 per cent cumulative growth rate in the installed capacity along with a purchase of power from central sector and other State Electricity Boards. Haryana's own generating capacity failed to keep pace with the expansion of peak demand as well as energy demand, which resulted in acute shortage of power in the state. The last generating unit, which was added to its own generating capacity, was of the 210 MW coal-based thermal power generation unit at Panipat in 1989. During the past eleven years (1987 to 1999), there was no addition to the generating capacity though energy demand has increased at

TABLE 3.3: SALIENT FEATURES OF THE POWER SYSTEM

| S. No. | Particulars | 1967–8 | 1980–1 | 1997–8 | Annual Compound Growth Rates | | |
|---|---|---|---|---|---|---|---|
| | | | | | 1967–8 to 1980–1 | 1980–1 to 1997–8 | 1967–8 to 1997–8 |
| 1. | Installed Capacity (MW) | | | | | | |
| | (a) Hydro | 368 (96.08) | 696 (59.34) | 1,106.30 (46.25) | 5.02 | 2.76 | 3.74 |
| | (b) Thermal | 15 (03.92) | 477 (40.66) | 1,285.70 (53.75) | 30.49 | 6.00 | 15.99 |
| | Total | 383 (100) | 1,173 (100) | 2,392 (100) | 8.99 | 4.28 | 6.29 |
| 2. | Actual Generation (M. KWh) | | | | | | |
| | (a) Hydro | 624.05 (96.14) | 2,460 (69.18) | 3,297.06 (46.29) | 11.12 | 1.74 | 5.71 |
| | (b) Thermal | 25.01 (03.86) | 1,096 (30.82) | 3,826.22 (53.71) | 33.74 | 7.63 | 18.25 |
| | Total | 649.60 (100) | 3,556 (100) | 7,123.28 (100) | 13.97 | 4.17 | 8.31 |
| 3. | Connected Load (MW) | 446.70 | 2,358 | 6,939.00 | 13.65 | 6.55 | 9.57 |
| 4. | Simultaneous Maximum Demand (MW) | 134 | 779 | 2,272 | 14.50 | 6.49 | 9.89 |
| 5. | Power Available for Sale (MU) | 649.64 | 4,184.00 | 13,303.06 | 15.40 | 7.04 | 10.58 |
| 6. | Energy Sale (MU) | 542.92 | 3,391.00 | 8,864.44 | 15.13 | 5.82 | 9.76 |
| 7. | T&D losses (MU) (percentage) | 106.78 (16.42%) | 793.00 (18.95%) | 4,438.62 (33.36%) | | | |
| 8. | LT and 11 KV Lines (Circuit Kilometres) | | | | | | |
| | (a) L.T. Lines | 9,796 | 66,493 | 105,266 | 14.66 | 2.59 | 7.70 |
| | (b) 11 KV Lines | 7,089 | 35,939 | 55,059 | 12.29 | 2.40 | 6.62 |
| | (c) No. of Transformers | 5,390 | 31,385 | 103,678 | 13.41 | 6.86 | 9.68 |
| 9. | Total No. of Connections | 311,914 | 1,093,630 | 3,422,926 | 10.13 | 6.20 | 7.78 |

*Source*: HSEB, *Annual Statement of Accounts*, Various years.

about a 10 per cent rate per annum. Haryana generated only one-third of its total consumption, about one-third was made available from its share in the Bhakra Beas systems, and the rest of the one-third it purchased from the central sector power companies. The overall energy shortage in the state was about 5 per cent and peak power shortage was about 20 per cent. Transmission and Distribution (T&D) losses in 1967–8 were 16.42 per cent of the total electricity supply and these were reported to have increased to 33.36 per cent in 1997–8. The estimates of T&D losses are not very reliable as most of the electricity supply to the agricultural sector is unmetered and consumption estimates for this sector are largely based on guesswork.

The transmission and distribution network in Haryana consists of 220 KV, 132 KV, 66 KV, and 33 KV transmission and transformation systems, and 11 KV and LT distribution systems. Up to 1979-80, the HSEB did not own even a single 220 KV substation. However, by 1996–7 it owned 15 such stations connected by 907 km. long transmission lines. During the period 1979–80 to 1996–7, all categories of transformation stations taken together increased from 191 to 402. The 132 KV substations increased from 28 to 71, 66 KV stations increased from 31 to 67, and 33 KV substations increased from 132 to 249. During the same period, the total length of transmission lines increased from 4,016 km. to 8,903 km., registering a growth rate of 5.96 per cent per annum. The electric power distribution system in Haryana consists of 11 KV and Low Tension (LT) and distribution transformers. Immediately after Haryana came into existence in 1966, the distribution network was expanded at a very impressive rate. In the period 1967–8 to 1980–1, LT lines, 11 KV lines, and the number of transformers registered annual growth rates of 14.66 per cent, 12.29 per cent and 13.41 per cent respectively. These growth rates declined to 2.59 per cent, 2.40 per cent and 6.86 per cent in the period 1980–1 to 1997–8.[2] Obviously, the investment in the distribution network was highly neglected in the second phase. Consequently, the distribution system was overloaded. This resulted in low voltage and in the frequent burning and tripping of the transformers.

## 2. ELECTRICITY CONSUMPTION PATTERNS

The rapid agrarian development in Haryana during the period of the Green Revolution generated a tremendous demand for power in the agricultural sector. Haryana being close to Delhi, the national capital, industrialization and urbanization spread at a relatively rapid pace in the areas located in the National Capital Region (NCR). Haryana agriculture is based on peasant proprietorship and, therefore, the increase in agriculutral productivity has enhanced the purchasing power of almost all sections of society which in turn gave a boost to the commercial activities in the state. The accelerated rate of growth in a wide range of economic activities was made possible by the very high growth in energy consumption by various categories of consumers.

The consumption of electricity in Haryana grew at quite a high rate, as is clear from Table 3.4. Total energy sale in the state grew at the rate of 12.66 per cent per annum in the period 1967–8 to 1980–1 (first phase), and 7.18 per cent during the period 1980–1 to 1998–9 (second phase). In the first phase, agricultural consumption registered the highest growth rate of 18.03 per cent, which was reduced to 8.35 per cent in the second phase, resulting in the overall growth over the whole period under consideration to be 12.30 per cent, which is really very impressive. Domestic consumption also registered growth rates of 15.25 per cent and 12.88 per cent in the first and second phases respectively. Electricity sale to the industrial sector grew at a rate of 10.31 per cent in the first phase, which declined to 2.42 per cent per annum in the second phase. Domestic, agricultural, and industrial consumption account for about 90 per cent of the total sale of electricity. However, significant differences in the growth rates of electricity sale to various consumer categories over the period under consideration has led to major changes in the relatives shares of electricity consumed by different categories of consumers. The share of domestic, industrial, and agricultural consumers in 1966–7 were 6.61 per cent, 62.70 per cent, and 20.36 per cent which changes to 22.59 per cent, 21.09 per cent and, 45.39 per cent respectively in 1998–9. The large proportionate increase in the sale of electricity to agricultural consumers is due to the preferential treatment given to agriculture, with minimum cuts during the periods of shortage. Due to severe cuts and poor reliability in supply to industrial consumers during the period of scarcity, industries have shifted more and more to the captive generation and consumption of power to ensure that their production does not suffer due to power cuts. This trend is wasteful and must be reversed.

Haryana has many significant achievements to its credit, as it was the first state in the country to achieve 100 per cent rural electrifica-

TABLE 3.4: ELECTRICITY CONSUMPTION IN HARYANA: RELATIVE SHARES AND GROWTH RATES

(*in lakh units*)

| S. No. | Consumer Class | 1967–8 | 1980–1 | 1998–9 | Annual Compound Growth Rates | | |
|---|---|---|---|---|---|---|---|
| | | | | | 1967–8 to 1980–1 | 1980–1 to 1998–9 | 1967–8 to 1998–9 |
| 1. | Domestic | 358.78 (6.61) | 2,271.95 (8.89) | 20,107.16 (22.59) | 15.25 | 12.88 | 13.87 |
| 2. | Commercial | 242.87 (4.47) | 729.54 (2.85) | 3,511.19 (3.95) | 8.82 | 9.12 | 9.00 |
| 3. | Industrial | 3,408.10 (62.70) | 12,202.01 (47.74) | 18,770.41 (21.09) | 10.31 | 2.42 | 5.66 |
| 4. | Agricultural | 1,105.42 (20.36) | 9,537.70 (37.32) | 40,396.58 (45.39 | 18.03 | 8.35 | 12.30 |
| 5. | Public Lighting | 32.27 (0.59) | 73.80 (0.29) | 300.45 (0.34) | 6.57 | 8.11 | 7.46 |
| 6. | Public Works | 34.91 (0.64) | 186.04 (0.73) | 2,385.18 (2.68) | 13.74 | 15.23 | 14.60 |
| 7. | Office/Workshops | 39.31 (0.72) | 64.61 (0.25) | 506.58 (0.57) | 3.92 | 12.12 | 8.60 |
| 8. | Bulk Supply | 207.51 (3.82) | 491.70 (1.52) | 3,021.54 (3.40) | 6.86 | 10.61 | 9.02 |
| 9. | Total | 5,429.17 (100.00) | 25,557.18 (100.00) | 88,999.09 (100) | 12.66 | 7.18 | 9.44 |

*Note*: Figures in parentheses are the relative shares of various consumer classes in electricity consumption in a particular year.
*Source*: Data collected from *Statistical Abstract of Haryana 1998–9*.

tion by electrifying all the 6,745 villages in the state in 1976–7. The per capita consumption of electricity in Haryana in 1996–7 was 504 units (Kwh) against the all-India average of 334 units, which gave it fourth position after the states of Punjab, Gujarat, and Maharashtra.[3] Though the achievements in terms of the physical expansion of the electric power system were quite impressive, the technical performance of the system remained a cause of concern. The overall capacity utilization of the thermal power plants, as reflected by the plant load factors, ranged between 32 per cent and 49 per cent (Table 3.5), while the plant availability was about 60 per cent. The forced outages were up to 30 per cent and the auxiliary consumption above 10 per cent. All these indicators clearly establish that the technical performance was quite unsatisfactory. T&D losses were also in a very high range, between 23 per cent and 33.36 per cent during the period 1987–8 to 1997–8.

We may conclude from the above analysis that the achievements in terms of the expansion in the generation, transmission, and distribution systems as well as the role of electric power in achieving high economic development have been quite impressive. However, the technical performance of the HSEB was not satisfactory and demand for electricity continuously outstripped supply, which rendered the physical infrastructure inadequate, overloading the existing system, resulting in voltage fluctuations and poor quality of supply.

TABLE 3.5: PLANT LOAD FACTORS

*(in per cent)*

| Year | PTPS | FTPS | Haryana State | India |
|---|---|---|---|---|
| 1980–1 | 32.60 | 30.00 | 32.30 | 41.60 |
| 1985–6 | 44.14 | 26.05 | 32.00 | 52.40 |
| 1990–1 | — | — | 34.50 | 53.09 |
| 1995–6 | 39.70 | 55.15 | 42.50 | 63.00 |
| 1996–7 | 48.36 | 44.92 | 47.70 | 64.40 |
| 1997–8 | 50.38 | 44.41 | 49.40 | 64.70 |
| 1998–9 (up to 14.8.1998) | 40.27 | 52.93 | 48.80 | 64.60 |

*Sources*: 1. HSEB, *Annual Statement of Accounts*, various issues.
2. Planning Commission, April 2000.

### 3. FINANCIAL PERFORMANCE OF HSEB

The financial position of the HSEB has been examined for the period 1990–1 to 1998–9. Two rates of return (ROR) have been computed: on the average capital base, one taking into account the subsidy provided by the state government and the other without it, as given in Table 3.6. The ROR, without taking into consideration the subsidy from the state government, ranged between –16.0 per cent and –47.79 per cent in the period under review. It may be noted that the performance in terms of the ROR consistently deteriorated from 1990–1 to 1997–8 as the ROR declined from –15.76 per cent to –47.79 per cent except for 1994–5. The state government was expected to provide subvention to the SEB for supplying electricity at a price lower than the cost of supply at the consumer's end. The board charged a lower tariff on the direction of the state government that wanted to achieve certain socio-economic or welfare objectives by making electricity available to certain consumer categories at prices lower than the cost of supply. Even after taking into consideration the subsidy given to the HSEB the ROR in 1990–1 to 1993–4 kept declining from –12.31 per cent to –27.5 per cent. In 1994–5 the ROR was –0.80 per cent and in the following two successive years 1995–6 and 1996–7 the ROR was positive (2.6 per cent and 0.41 per cent respectively) as the state government compensated the board completely. It may be noted that commercial losses without subsidy kept increasing from Rs. 164.76 crore in 1990–1 to Rs. 725 crore in 1997–8. However, commercial losses after taking into account the subvention from the state government showed a declining trend after 1993–4 as the state government subventions in 1993–4 was Rs. 60 crore and it was increased to Rs. 631.6 crore in 1996–7.[4]

The above analysis clearly brings out that though in principle the state is expected to compensate the SEBs for meeting its socio-economic commitments, the state government failed to discharge its responsibility to financially compensate the electricity board. Such an arbitrary interference also makes the management and administration complacent as well as despondent, leaving little motivation or desire to improve the administration or increase the technical efficiency.

It will be quite helpful to examine the pricing policy in relation to the financial performance of the HSEB. To examine the pricing policy of the HSEB in relation to the cost of supplying power, a separate analysis has been carried out for each consumer class with a view to

TABLE 3.6: FINANCIAL PERFORMANCE

| S. No. | Particulars | 1990–1 | 1991–2 | 1992–3 | 1993–4 | 1994–5 | 1995–6 | 1996–7 | 1997–8 (Prov.) | 1998–9 (RE) |
|---|---|---|---|---|---|---|---|---|---|---|
| 1. | ROR Without Subsidy (%) | –15.96 | –19.24 | –26.10 | –31.20 | 27.90 | 31.80 | 38.35 | –47.79 | –33.27 |
| 2. | ROR With Subsidy (%) | –12.31 | –16.44 | –23.80 | –27.50 | –0.80 | 2.60 | 0.41 | –2.02 | –10.52 |
| 3. | Commercial Losses Without Subsidy (Rs. in Crores) | 164.76 | 275.38 | –403.60 | –506.90 | –468 | –554 | –625 | –725 | –532 |
| 4. | Commercial Losses With Subsidy (Rs. in Crores) | 128.71 | –235.35 | –368.40 | –446.90 | –13 | 46 | 7 | –32 | –168 |
| 5. | State Subsidy (Rs. in Crores) | 36.05 | 40.03 | 35.20 | 60.00 | 455 | 599.70 | 631.60 | 732.40 | 364 |

*Sources*: 1. HSEB: *Annual Statement of Accounts*, various issues.
2. Planning Commission, *Annual Report on the Working of State Electricity Boards and Electricity Departments*, April 2000.

determining the nature of the relationship between the average revenue realized from the various consumer categories within the state and the average cost of supplying power. It will help us to bring out the extent to which energy sale to each consumer class involves profit earning or subsidization. The analysis is confined to the period 1985–6 to 1997–8.

Most of the State Electricity Boards follow the average cost based pricing principle. The actual tariff is worked out by the application of certain rules of the thumb, keeping an eye on the average cost of supply, the capacity of the consumers to bear the burden, and certain other socio-economic considerations. The consumers have been grouped into various categories on the basis of the nature of use and type of demand. The major categories of consumers are: (i) domestic supply, (ii) commercial supply, (iii) agricultural supply, (iv) small industrial supply, (v) medium industrial power supply, (vi) large industrial power supply, (vii) street lighting, (viii) public works and sewerage, (ix) bulk supply.

The cost of supplying power depends on the following principal factors: (i) quantity of energy supplied, (ii) maximum demand, (iii) load factor, (iv) diversity factor, (v) location, (vi) time of load incidence, (vii) seasonal variations of load, and (viii) power factor. The cost of power supply increases with an increase in the geographical distance of the consumers from the power-generating station due to an increase in the transmission and distribution costs. However, in actual tariff formulation these differences are ignored, as it is an accepted norm that everybody in a region has a right to receive the supply at the same price if the nature of the load is the same. The price charged from high capacity demanding consumers is normally based on a two-part tariff. One part, called 'demand charges', is related to the maximum demand or connected load of the consumers, and the other is related to the amount of energy consumed on the kilo-watt-hour (unit) basis. From the small consumers, the price is charged on the basis of per unit of energy consumed. Another component of the price charged is the electricity duty imposed by the state government.

The average revenue realized from the electricity sale within the state to various consumer categories and the average cost of electricity supply is presented in Table 3.7. The analysis of the results provides an interesting insight into the dynamics of tariff making in Haryana over time. On technical grounds, the cost of electricity sup-

TABLE 3.7: CONSUMER CLASS-WISE AVERAGE REVENUE AND AVERAGE COST OF SUPPLY

(*Paise per unit*)

| S. No. | Description | 1985–6 | 1990–1 | 1991–2 | 1992–3 | 1993–4 | 1994–5 | 1995–6 | 1996–7 | 1997–8 |
|---|---|---|---|---|---|---|---|---|---|---|
| 1. | Domestic | 41.10 | 61.09 | 67.80 | 70.11 | 76.91 | 100.48 | 133.46 | 169.00 | 203.95 |
| | | (57.40) | (58.91) | (58.70) | (52.20) | (46.60) | (56.00) | (63.95) | (67.63) | (69.51) |
| 2. | Commercial | 62.89 | 133.05 | 139.50 | 149.61 | 175.05 | 209.99 | 253.24 | 300.45 | 338.27 |
| | | (87.90) | (128.41) | (120.80) | (111.30) | (106.00) | (116.97) | (121.35) | (121.69) | (115.29) |
| 3. | Small Power, | 48.96 | 113.69 | 129.52 | 149.85 | 170.68 | 207.42 | 256.58 | 326.40 | 381.59 |
| | Low and Medium | (68.40) | (109.70) | (112.20) | (111.50) | (103.40) | (115.53) | (122.95 | (130.62) | (153.00) |
| 4. | Industrial HT | 77.44 | 42.93 | 162.32 | 179.27 | 206.18 | 227.89 | 270.38 | 317.41 | 368.09 |
| | | (108.20) | (137.91) | (140.60) | (133.40) | (124.90) | (126.94) | (162.68) | (127.02) | (125.46) |
| 5. | Public Lighting | 63.18 | 98.21 | 109.53 | 105.25 | 105.27 | 168.17 | 191.66 | 248.87 | 344.49 |
| | | (88.30) | (94.70) | (94.90) | (178.30) | (63.70) | (93.67) | (129.56) | (99.59) | (117.41) |
| 6. | Irrigation | 19.95 | 20.51 | 16.18 | 21.97 | 28.98 | 45.38 | 51.93 | 52.41 | 61.08 |
| | | (27.90) | (19.80) | (14.00) | (16.30) | (17.60) | (25.28) | (24.88) | (20.97) | (20.82) |
| 7. | Public Works | 48.96 | 102.98 | 130.39 | 144.10 | 164.80 | 198.04 | 266.31 | 310.38 | 356.90 |
| | | (64.40) | (99.30) | (112.90) | (107.20) | (88.80) | (110.31) | (127.61) | (124.20) | (121.64) |
| 8. | Average Revenue | 41.70 | 66.63 | 66.13 | 72.54 | 83.34 | 110.81 | 132.76 | 155.28 | 187.36 |
| | from Sale within State | (58.30) | (64.30) | (57.40) | (54.00) | (50.50) | (61.72) | (63.62) | (62.14) | (63.86) |
| 9. | Average Cost of Supply | 71.57 | 103.66 | 115.47 | 134.40 | 165.10 | 179.53 | 208.69 | 249.89 | 293.40 |

*Note*: Figures in parentheses represent average per unit reveune as a percentage of average unit cost oc electricity supply in a particular year.

*Sources*: HSEB, *Annual Statement of Accounts, 1985–6 to 1999–2000.*

ply at the higher voltage levels is lower; the cost of electricity supply at the lower voltage levels is higher. Similarly, the cost of electricity supply in densely populated areas is lower than in the thinly populated areas as transmission and distribution costs and service charges per consumer will be lower. As per the pricing policy of the HSEB, various categories of consumers are charged tariff at different rates. This is clearly reflected in the average revenue realized in a particular year from different consumer categories. Table 3.7 indicates that normally commercial consumers were charged tariff rates consistently at higher rates than the domestic consumers. Similarly, big industrial (HT) consumers were charged at higher rates in comparison to the small and medium industrial consumers. Agricultural consumers were priced the lowest, though the cost of supply to them is the highest. This implies that tariff rates do not have any systematic relationship with the cost of supply. Capacity to bear the cost and some other socio-economic and political considerations appear to have played a dominant role in the formation of the tariff structure.

A comparison of the average revenue realized from the electricity sold within the state and the average cost of supply shows that over the period under consideration the overall average revenue increased from 41.70 paise per unit in 1985–6 to 187.36 paise per unit in 1997–8. The average cost of supply in the corresponding period increased from 71.57 paise per unit to 293.40 paise per unit respectively. It clearly brings out that the price per unit of electricity sold did increase over time but it was inadequate to meet the cost, whereby the average revenue realized was consistently lower than the cost of supplying electricity though the shortfall did decline. There was not even a single year in which the average revenue was higher than the average cost of electricity supply. Figures in the brackets are the average revenue as a proportion of the average cost of supplying electricity (AR/AC) in percentage terms. It shows that in 1985–6, the average revenue was 58.3 per cent of the average cost. In the first half of the 1990s, the average revenue as a proportion of the average cost of supply declined, but since 1994–5 it consistently increased because of a steep increase in the tariff of commercial and industrial consumers. The average revenue realized from domestic consumers also increased significantly. The increase in tariff rates did not appear to have any logical relationship to the cost of supply to various consumer classes.[5] The only criterion appeared to be the capacity to pay without much political fallout. This behaviour pattern indicates that there is no economic rationality in the pricing policy. Tariff rates were revised when financial crises reached a flash point, then the situation was allowed to drift for the next one or two years. As the fixing of the tariff rates was a political decision dictated by the government, there did not appear to be any serious attempt to achieve the statutory financial requirements or even the break-even point. The financial loss or surplus from the sale of electricity to various categories of consumers is presented in Table 3.8. It clearly shows that revenue loss due to subsidized supply in 1985–6 was Rs. 82.12 crore and it increased to Rs. 874.5 crore in 1997–8.

The total quantum of subsidy to domestic consumers was Rs. 14.81 crore in 1985–6 and it kept increasing consistently up to 1993–4 when it rose to Rs. 136.67 crore. In 1994–5, it declined to Rs. 114.28 crore. However, in the following years it again showed an increasing trend and in 1997–8 it rose to Rs. 162.91 crore. The commercial tariff consistently generated a surplus over time. Industrial consumers were not subsidized and they significantly contributed to the surplus of the HSEB. Public lighting has also being consistently subsidized. The tariff of electricity supply to public works and sewerage was lower than the supply for public lighting up to 1990–1. It was raised subsequently and became higher than the cost of supply, thus contributing to surplus generation.

An analysis of the pricing policy for tube-well irrigation presents a picture in sharp contrast. The average revenue realized from agricultural consumers recovers only 20 per cent of the cost of supply. As the total electricity consumption by agriculture ranged from 35 per cent to 45 per cent of the total sale within the state, the amount of subsidy increased from Rs. 70.54 crore in 1985–6 to Rs. 892.72 crore in 1997–8.

The above analysis of the financial performance of the HSEB for the period 1985–6 to 1997–8 brings out that the performance has been highly unsatisfactory. During this period, domestic consumers and irrigations pump sets were the two major groups of consumers that were highly subsidized.

## 4. TRANSMISSION AND DISTRIBUTION LOSSES

The transmission and distribution losses as a proportion of electric energy available for sale in Haryana is presented in Table 3.9.

An analysis of the estimates of T&D losses brings out a very

TABLE 3.8: CONSUMER CLASS-WISE AVERAGE SURPLUS/SUBSIDY

(*Rs. in crore*)

| S. No. | Particulars | 1985–6 | 1990–1 | 1991–2 | 1992–3 | 1993–4 | 1994–5 | 1995–6 | 1996–7 | 1997–8 |
|---|---|---|---|---|---|---|---|---|---|---|
| 1. | Domestic | –14.81 | –48.46 | –61.58 | –95.51 | –136.67 | –114.28 | –123.17 | –145.13 | –162.91 |
| 2. | Non Domestic/ Commercial | –0.64 | +5.14 | +4.91 | +3.45 | +2.21 | +7.32 | +11.48 | +14.57 | +14.20 |
| 3. | Small Power, Low and Medium Power | –5.59 –1.29 | +4.80 | +7.029 | +8.31 | +5.05 | +15.38 | +26.30 | +42.88 | +52.00 |
| 4. | HT Industrial | +5.29 | +49.74 | +59.37 | +61.77 | +49.79 | +65.27 | +90.54 | +93.63 | +100.41 |
| 5. | Public Lighting | –0.126 | –0.13 | –0.154 | –1.072 | –2.91 | –0.45 | –0.68 | –0.37 | +1.60 |
| 6. | Irrigation | –70.54 | –225.48 | –350.72 | –456.77 | –538.91 | -492.55 | –612 | –806.53 | +892.77 |
| 7. | Public Works and Sewerage | N.A. | –30.057 | +1.45 | +1.17 | –0.05 | +2.98 | +10 | +12.01 | +13.38 |
| 8. | Total Surplus Loss | –82.12 | –214.45 | –339.70 | –478.65 | –620.89 | –516.33 | –597.53 | –788.60 | –874.50 |

*Source*: Computed from data collected from various issues of *HSEB: Annual Statement of Accounts*.

TABLE 3.9: TRANSMISION AND DISTRIBUTION LOSSES

| S. No. | Period | Range in percentage |
|---|---|---|
| 1. | 1968–9 to 1971–2 | 22 to 29 |
| 2. | 1972–3 to 1986–7 | 14 to 19 |
| 3. | 1987–8 to 1994–5 | 24 to 28 |
| 4. | 1995–6 to 1997–8 | 31 to 34 |

*Sources*: 1. *Statistical Abstract of Haryana 1995–6*, pp. 428–9.
2. Planning Commission, April 2000, p. 66.

erratic picture. In the initial years of the existence of the HSEB, T&D losses from 1968–9 to 1971–2 were in the range of 22 per cent to 29 per cent. In the period, 1972–3 to 1986–7, they declined to the range of 14 per cent to 19 per cent. Then in the next period from 1987–8 to 1994–5, the losses rose to the range of 24 per cent to 28 per cent, and thereafter during 1995–6 to 1997–8, the losses further increased to the range of 31 per cent to 34 per cent.[6] Reduction in T&D losses in the 1970s may have been because the T&D system was not overloaded. However, after 1977 when the flat rate system for agricultural supply was introduced and metering was discontinued, the rate of agricultural consumption was an estimate based on certain norms regarding the numbers of hours for which tube-wells were operated and amout of the sanctioned load, etc. Soon the management, with the active connivance of the political bosses, discovered that the account of agricultural consumption was a black box into which its inefficiency, the extent of pilferage of power, etc., could be transferred without any accountability. Therefore, the estimates of T&D losses became a policy decision. Since the early 1990s, it appears to be a conscious decision on the part of both the political leadership and the management to show much higher T&D losses, including theft of power, to provide legitimacy to the programme of reforms and privatization.

The rehabilitation of the electric power system in Haryana required huge investments, including for the renovation and modernization of the existing thermal power plant in order to expand its generating capacity to enlarge the transmission and distribution system. As the required finances were not forthcoming, the Haryana government decided to take a loan of $ 600 million from the World Bank. In fact, Haryana is the second state after Orissa to undertake power sector reforms under the supervision of the World Bank. Here, we will confine ourselves to an analysis of the actual experience of the reforms process.

## 5. EXPERIENCE OF THE ELECTRICITY REFORM PROCESS

The Haryana State Assembly passed the Haryana Electricity Reforms Act on 22 July 1997. After the getting President of India's consent, the Gazette Notification was issued on 10 March 1998 and the Haryana Electricity Reforms Act, 1997 came into force with effect from 14 August 1998. The Haryana State Electricity Board has been restructured and the following companies have been created. All the electricity generation functions have been transferred to the Haryana Power Generation Corporation (HPGC). Transmission and bulk supply functions have been transferred to the Haryana Vidyut Prasaran Nigam Limited (HVPNL). For the distribution business, two distribution companies have been constituted, namely, the Uttar Haryana Bijli Vitran Nigam (UHBVN) and the Dakshin Haryana Bijli Vitran Nigam (DHBVN).

To regulate the activities of the transmission and distribution companies in the state, the Haryana Electricity Regulatory Commission (HERC) has been created. The Commission is required to act as a vanguard of the interests of all the stakeholders in the electric power system: the consumers, the power producers, and the transmission as well as the distribution companies. It is also expected to promote competition and efficiency in the industry and also to facilitate the sustained development of the power sector in the state. The Commission has issued guidelines as regards the conduct of its business, its tariff philosophy, and guidelines for load forecast, resource plans, and the power procurement process.[7] As per the Electricity Reforms Act, 1997, the transmission and distribution companies are required to file their Annual Revenue Requirement (ARR) and their proposed tariff increases for the next financial year by 31 December of the current year to enable the Commission to pass orders before the commencement of the next financial year. The Commission is expected to follow a transparent decision-making process before passing its order. The Commission is required to hold public hearings and give opportunities to various stakeholders, the public (consumers), and the licensees to present their views.[8]

It was for the first time in the history of the electricity industry in

Haryana that the transmission and distribution companies were required to provide complete information regarding the various parameters to evaluate their technical and financial performance during FY 2000–1. As the quality of the information provided was not adequate, the Commission directed the transmission and distribution companies to submit additional information three times. Though the quantity and quality of information was not up to the mark to evaluate the technical and financial performance precisely, the process did bring out the gaps in the information that needed to be bridged. The Commission did allow waivers in the supply of information this time and directed the companies to submit all the required information while filing the ARRs for the next financial year.

The HVPNL filed its first ARR in December 1998 and the second ARR in 31 December 2000 for the FY 2000–1.[9] Some of the findings of the Commission are very illuminating.

The exact amount of power received from the BBMB power station was not known as the HVPNL (also the erstwhile HSEB) did not have a metering arrangement at the receiving points in Haryana. In the absence of interface meters at the transmission and distribution interface, it is not possible to know the actual level of the transmission losses. As the supply is mostly unmetered, the HVPNL has estimated that free supply to its employees and offices and its own works may be 63.55 Million Units (MU), which is not metered. About 80 per cent of the agricultural supply is unmetered and is supplied at a flat rate. In such a situation, the evaluation of the technical performance is not possible. The HERC directed the HVPNL in November 1999 that it must install meters at the transmission and distribution interface and it promised to do so by December 2000. However, it failed to honour its commitment and asked for an extension up to June 2001. The HERC reluctantly agreed and directed the HPVNL to complete the interface metering by 31 July 2001 positively, otherwise it would attract some punishment. The Commission has directed the HVPNL and its subsidiaries to replace all defective meters by 31 July 2001. The government of Haryana has accepted the Minimum Action Plan and has committed to meter all agricultural pump set connections by the end of 2001.

Metering is the foremost task to ensure transparency in the functioning of the system. The absence of a metering of T&D losses—apparently a part of the management's policy—has become, rather scandalous. Before the reform process was initiated, the general tendency on the part of the management was to underestimate T&D losses and to transfer the losses, including the pilferage of power, to the agricultural consumption account which served a double purpose. It enabled the political leadership to project that it was supplying 40–5 per cent of the total supply to the agricultural sector and thus it was pro-*kisan*. At the same time it came in handy to the management to conceal their inefficiency and to evade accountability.

As a result of such an active connivance among the vested interests, up to the early 1990s, the HSEB used to project that its T&D losses were about 20 per cent. Then to provide legitimacy to the reform process and to discredit the existing institutional set-up, the management and the political leadership informed the people that T&D losses had increased to about 35 per cent and that reforms were inevitable to improve technical performance and to escape from financial bankruptcy. No questions were asked her nor any accountability fixed for the previous mess. While passing orders on the ARR for 1999–2000, the HERC reluctantly allowed 36.56 per cent T&D losses for financial calculations. However, it directed the HVPNL to reduce them to 24.69 per cent, including distribution losses of 16.69 per cent. During 2000–1, the T&D losses did not show any decline. The Commission has estimated that T&D losses in Haryana were 40.76 per cent, out of which 7.76 per cent were transmission losses and 35.77 per cent were distribution losses. To bring to an end the game of 'your guess is as good as my guess', the adoption of both statutory metering and monitoring of power is indispensable. Society must act as a watchdog, otherwise vested interests shall also scuttle this plan of action or at least delay it as far as possible.

There are certain other startling facts that need to be highlighted. Arrears of receivables (dues) on 14 August 1998, when the HSEB was restructured, were Rs. 758.64 crores and by 31 March 2000, the arrears had increased to Rs. 986.50 crore. This shows that the performance of the HVPNL for the first 19 months of the restructuring process had in fact deteriorated and had added to the unrecovered dues by Rs. 227.87 crore, which is an increase of 30 per cent! What is no less intriguing is that the unpaid dues of the government offices were Rs. 132.77 crore out of a total of Rs. 986.50 crore. Obviously, such a performance in collection indicates deteriorating efficiency in the collection of dues, and this poses a serious threat to the financial viability of the distribution licensee.

The HVPNL has estimated that free supply was 63.55 MU, out of which 21.79 MU was the supply to its offices and other work places and the rest of the 41.76 MU were free supplies to its employees. The HERC estimated that in case of distribution companies, these concessions amount to 16 per cent of the total Administration & General expenditure and 5.7 per cent of the basic salaries of the employees respectively. Any concession given must be transparent and its implications should be defendable. A very alarming finding of the Commission appears to be that the load factor of small (LT) industrial consumers is abnormally low, which implies that they use electricity on an average 2.06 hours per day. It signals a case for the large-scale pilferage of power. The Commission has rightly recommended that the meters of all LT industries should be checked by an independent agency in order to plug leakages of substantial revenue, which appears to be taking place.

The HERC's arguments to enhance the tariff for domestic consumers seem to defy any socio-economic rationality. The HVPNL had proposed that tariff be raised by 11 paise from 191 paise per unit to 202 paise per unit. However, the Commission has ordered a three slab based tariff: for the first 40 units consumption @ 260 paise per unit, for the next 260 units at 360 paise per unit, and for consumption above 300 units @ 425 paise per unit. The rationale provided by the Commission is that its cost of service study shows that the cost of supply to domestic consumers was 451 paise per unit. The Commission has not been fair to the domestic consumers as while computing the cost of service, the average T&D losses assumed were 40.76 per cent, out of which the transmission losses were 7.76 per cent and the distribution system losses were 35.77 per cent. While filing the ARR, the Commission had asked the HVPNL to make its calculations after taking the distribution losses to be of the order of 16.69 per cent. This means that genuine domestic consumers have been penalized and have been asked to pay for the pilferage of the order of 15 per cent to 20 per cent. On top of this, the HERC has argued that domestic consumers are still being subsidized by 85 paise per unit as the average revenue realization from the new tariff will be 312 paise per unit against the cost of 451 paise per unit. The arguments of the Commission are not fair. The tariff rates for commercial consumers have been kept unchanged at 419 paise per unit. For HT industrial consumers, the tariff has been reduced as they get supply at a higher voltage for which the cost of supply is lower.

For metered supply to the agricultural sector, the Commission has accepted the proposal of the licensee to allow a tariff increase of 12 paise per unit, whereas for flat rates supply the Commission has accepted the government of Haryana's request to reduce the tariff rates due to the drought situation in lieu of which the government has agreed to provide an additional subsidy of Rs. 413 crore in addition to the already committed subvention of Rs. 412 crore. We think it is fair enough so long as it does not adversely affect the finances of the licensee.

The approved ARR for the distribution business for FY 2000–1 was Rs. 3,730.44 crore and the new tariff was estimated to fetch Rs. 2,738.11 crore over the full one-year, leaving a gap of Rs. 992.33 crore (only three months of FY 2000–1 were left when the order was implemented). It is estimated that for FY 2000–1, the gap between the allowed ARR and the revenue realized through the new tariff will be Rs. 1,292 crore. After taking into account the government subsidy for the concessional supply to the agricultural sector of Rs. 613.08 crore and the deferred liability of Rs. 156.22 crore, the deficit of Rs. 432 crore still remains uncovered. Rs. 259.2 crore was allowed as deferred cost for which borrowings were allowed and the licensee had been asked to make up Rs. 172.8 crore through efficiency gains. The Commission has allowed the HVPNL to borrow from the market but this will add to the interest liabilities for which genuine consumers will have to pay in future. This expedient option is not justified beyond a point.

The regulatory process has underlined the weak spots and deficiencies in the data system management of the utilities/licensees. The restructured companies remain effectively under the control of the state bureaucracy. To change the mindset of the management of the utilities, professional will have to be inducted at the higher levels of management and functional autonomy will have to be ensured. The Commission has followed a persuasive path while underlining the inefficiencies and inadequacies in the technical and financial aspects. But there is an inherent conflict in the interests of the political leadership, the bureaucracy, the licensees, and the consumers. The public organizations will have to act as watchdogs and actively participate in the regulatory process.

The above analysis of the technical and financial performance of the erstwhile HSEB and the regulatory process in Haryana clearly brings out that unless T&D losses are brought down to acceptable levels by improving the technical efficiency and by checking the theft of power, it will not be possible to ensure an adequate investment in the power sector. And there can be no argument with the assertion that adequate supply of electricity is a precondition to the economic development of the state and is essential for the improvement in the quality of life of the people.

## NOTES

1. Economic and Statistical Organization, *Statistical Abstract of Haryana 1998–9*, Planning Department, Government of Haryana, 2000.
2. Based on information collected from various *Annual Administration Reports of the Haryana State Electricity Board.*
3. (a) Ministry of Finance, *Economic Survey 2000–1*, 2001; (b) Planning Commission, *Annual Report on the Working of State Electricity Boards and Electricity Departments*, 2000.
4. Electricity is supplied to various categories of consumers at different voltages. The higher the voltage of supply, the lower will be the cost of supply (see Surinder Kumar, 1984). The HSEB does not calculate the cost of supply at various voltages. Here, a comparison has been made with the average cost of supply of the whole system.
5. T&D losses data for various years is collected from the *Annual Statement of Accounts, and Annual Administration Reports* for various years published by the HSEB.
6. T&D loss data for different years is as per *Annual Statement of Accounts* and *Annual Administrative Reports* of the PSEB.
7. Haryana Electricity Regulatory Commission, Consultation Paper II: *Issues of Tariff Philosophy*, Panchkula, Haryana, 1999.
8. (i) Haryana Electricity Regulatory Commission, *Guidelines for Filing of Annual Revenue Reports,* 1999.
   (ii) Haryana Government Gazette (Extraordinary), 10 March 1998: *The Haryana Electricity Reform Act*, 1997.
9. Haryana Electricity Regulatory Commission, *Commission's Order on Annual Revenue Requirement for Transmission and Bulk Supply Business for 2000–1*, and *Transmission and Bulk Supply Tariff*, 14 December 2000, and *Order on ARR & Tariff for Distribution and Retail Supply*, 22 December 2000.

CHAPTER 4

# Perceptions of Punjab Consumers Regarding Theft of Power

In the last two chapters the technical and financial performance of the Punjab State Electricity Board and the erstwhile Haryana State Electricity Board have been analysed. They also contained some discussion on transmission and distribution (T&D) losses, extent of power theft and the remedial measures taken by the State Electricity Boards to curb the mischief of power theft in the states. Then next issue in hand was obtaining the perceptions of consumers and employees. As such a questionnaire was prepared and circulated among a representative sample of consumers and employees.

## SAMPLING DESIGN

Historically, Punjab can be divided into three distinct regions—Majha, Doaba, and Malwa. The Majha region consists of eleven districts, namely, Ludhiana, Ferozpur, Bhatinda, Mansa, Barnala, Rupnagar, Faridkot, Sirhind, Patiala, Muktsar, and Moga. The Doaba region consists of four districts, namely Jalandhar, Kapurthala, Hoshiarpur, and Nawan Shehar. The Malwa region consists of two districts, namely Amritsar and Gurdaspur. These regions differ in terms of the level of economic development, industrialization, and other socio-economic features. These regions broadly coincide with the levels of agricultural development.

We have employed a stratified purposive sampling design to collect data with the help of structured schedules for the consumers of various categories and for the employees holding different positions in the electricity distribution system.

For the survey three districts, namely Amritsar from the Malwa Region (Region I), Jalandhar from the Doaba Region (Region II), Rupnagar from the Majha Region (Region III), were selected. Each district was further sub-divided into urban and rural areas. The distribution of respondent consumers selected from the urban and rural areas of the selected districts is presented in Table 4.1.

A total sample of 249 respondent consumers was selected out of whom 90 were domestic consumers, 30 each were commercial, agricultural, small power, medium power and large power consumers, 6 were bulk supply consumers, and 3 were public lighting consumers.

Similarly, a total of 99 respondent employees were selected. The regional distribution of the various categories of employees in the sample is presented in Table 4.2.

For interview schedules of the consumers and employees, separate code manuals were developed to codify the data for computer processing. From the codified data the required frequency tables were generated and subjected to analysis.

TABLE 4.1 REGIONAL DISTRIBUTION OF RESPONDENT CONSUMERS

| Category | Region 1 | | Region 2 | | Region 3 | | Total |
|---|---|---|---|---|---|---|---|
| | Urban | Rural | Urban | Rural | Urban | Rural | |
| Domestic | 15 | 15 | 15 | 15 | 15 | 15 | 90 |
| Commercial | 5 | 5 | 5 | 5 | 5 | 5 | 30 |
| Agricultural | — | 10 | — | 10 | — | 10 | 30 |
| Small Power | 5 | 5 | 5 | 5 | 5 | 5 | 30 |
| Medium Power | 5 | 5 | 5 | 5 | 5 | 5 | 30 |
| Large Power | 5 | 5 | 5 | 5 | 5 | 5 | 30 |
| Bulk Supply | 2 | — | 2 | — | 2 | — | 6 |
| Street Lighting | 1 | 0 | 1 | 0 | 1 | 0 | 3 |
| Total | 38 | 45 | 38 | 45 | 38 | 45 | 249 |

TABLE 4.2 REGIONAL DISTRIBUTION OF RESPONDENT EMPLOYEES

| Category | Region 1 | Region 2 | Region 3 | Total |
|---|---|---|---|---|
| SE | 1 | 1 | 1 | 3 |
| XEN | 2 | 2 | 2 | 6 |
| SDO | 4 | 4 | 4 | 12 |
| JE | 6 | 6 | 6 | 18 |
| Lineman | 10 | 10 | 10 | 30 |
| Meter Reader | 10 | 10 | 10 | 30 |
| Total | 33 | 33 | 33 | 99 |

## ANALYSIS OF CONSUMER'S PERCEPTIONS

Now our discussion will focus on the perceptions of consumers by analysing their response patterns. These perceptions relate to their attitude towards the menace of power theft and conservation of energy, their knowledge of various methods used for the pilferage of power and methods to check it, their views regarding the efficacy of the existing organizational structure, accountability, responsiveness, etc., the community-based intervention strategies to combat the evil of theft and pilferage of power, and finally the perceptions of agricultural consumers regarding the use of tube well connections. Accordingly, the analysis of the consumers' perceptions has been divided into six sections.

Section 1 deals with perceptions and attitude of consumers towards the problem of power theft and conservation of energy.

Section 2 discusses the knowledge of the various methods used by people to pilfer power and the methods to check this malpractice.

Section 3 deals with people's perceptions regarding the existing tariff rates, the tariff structure, etc.

Section 4 deals with perceptions about the efficacy of the existing organizational structure, accountability, responsiveness, etc.

Section 5 deals with perceptions regarding community-based intervention strategies to combat the evil of the pilferage of power.

Section 6 deals with the perceptions of agricultural consumers (farmers) regarding the use of tube well connections.

### 1. *Attitudes towards Power Theft*

Consumers were asked about the problems faced by them in relation to the supply of electricity. Respondents were asked to state four major problems faced by them. Low voltage of electricity was identified as the most important problem faced by the majority of consumers (51 per cent), which included 56 per cent of domestic consumers, 53 per cent of commercial consumers, 70 per cent of agricultural consumers, 50 per cent of small power consumers, 43 per cent of medium power consumers, 27 per cent of large power consumers, and 33 per cent each of bulk supply and street lighting consumers. This was followed by irregular supply/frequent break-downs/trippings (46 per cent) and inadequate supply of electricity (32 per cent). About 26 per cent of consumers could not identify the major problems faced by them and responded by answering that they did not have any problem (Table 4.3).

Consumers were asked whether the employees of PSEB were cooperative in the quick redressal of their complaints. A majority of consumers (63 per cent) mentioned that the employees were cooperative. They included 66 per cent of domestic consumers, 60 per cent each of commercial, agricultural, and small power consumers, 63 per cent of medium power consumers, 70 per cent of large power consumers, 50 per cent of bulk supply consumers and 67 per cent of street lighting consumers. About 30 per cent of the consumers were of the view that the employees were not very cooperative and that repeated follow-ups had to be done. A few consumers (7 per cent) found the employees to be absolutely non-cooperative.

The various problems in relation to the supply of electricity such as low voltage, frequent trippings, power cuts, etc., are manifested in the poor quality of the service provided to the consumers. To assess the level of awareness of the respondent consumers regarding the reasons for the quality of the electricity supply, they were asked the reasons for the poor quality of service. It is interesting to note that most of the consumers (61 per cent) knew that along with the shortage of supply, the major reason for the low voltage and the frequent breakdown of supply was the overloading of the transformers, which get burnt out frequently. This was followed by the poor maintenance of the distribution network (23 per cent) and the shortage of maintenance staff (19 per cent) (Table 4.4).

To determine the level of awareness regarding the unnecessary/wasteful use of power and the energy conservation methods/technologies, the respondent consumers were asked questions regarding the ways in which consumers waste power. Their perceptions are shown in Table 4.5. An overwhelming majority of consumers (91 per cent) attributed the wastage of power by consumers to unnecessary use of electricity, followed by the use of appliances of higher wattage than was required (49 per cent). About 10 per cent of the respondents attributed avoidable wastage to the desire to show off at social ceremonies. Only 12 per cent respondents showed an awareness that electricity could be saved by energy-efficient technologies. This perception of consumers implies that a large number of people lack the knowledge of energy conservation measures. So there is an urgent need to create awareness among consumers of the social value/cost involved in the wasting of energy. In other words, the motivation and

TABLE 4.3: PROBLEMS FACED BY CONSUMERS IN RELATION TO SUPPLY OF ELECTRICITY

| Category of Consumer | Inadequate Supply | Low Voltage | Irregular Supply/ Frequent Breakdown/ Tripping | Any Other | No Problem | Total Respondents |
|---|---|---|---|---|---|---|
| Domestic | 26<br>(28.89) | 50<br>(55.56) | 45<br>(50.00) | 3<br>(3.33) | 22<br>(24.44) | 90<br>(100.00) |
| Commercial | 3<br>(10.00) | 16<br>(53.33) | 16<br>(53.33) | 0 | 12<br>(40.00) | 30<br>(100.00) |
| Agricultural | 18<br>(60.00) | 21<br>(70.00) | 21<br>(70.00) | 0 | 2<br>(6.67) | 30<br>(100.00) |
| Small Power | 12<br>(40.00) | 15<br>(50.00) | 8<br>(26.67) | 3<br>(10.00) | 9<br>(30.00) | 30<br>(100.00) |
| Medium Power | 10<br>(33.33) | 13<br>(43.33) | 11<br>(36.67) | 0<br>(0.00) | 4<br>(13.33) | 30<br>(100.00) |
| Large Power | 10<br>(33.33) | 8<br>(26.67) | 10<br>(33.33) | 1<br>(3.33) | 13<br>(43.33) | 30<br>(100.00) |
| Bulk Supply | 0<br>0.00 | 2<br>(33.33) | 2<br>(33.33) | 0<br>(0.00) | 3<br>(50.00) | 6<br>(100.00) |
| Street Lighting | 2<br>(66.67) | 1<br>(33.33) | 2<br>(66.67) | 1<br>(33.33) | 0 | 3<br>(100.00) |
| Total | 81<br>(32.53) | 126<br>(50.60) | 115<br>(46.18) | 8<br>(3.21) | 65<br>(26.10) | 249<br>(100.00) |

*Note*: Figures in parentheses show percentages.
*Source*: Field Survey.

TABLE 4.4: REASONS FOR THE POOR QUALITY OF SERVICE OF ELECTRICTY TO CONSUMERS

| Category of Consumer | Inadequate Supply | Overloading of trans- formers | Poor maintenance of Distri- bution Network | Shortage of Maint- enance Staff | Total No. of Respondents |
|---|---|---|---|---|---|
| Domestic | 14 | 53 | 18 | 17 | 90 |
| | (15.56) | (58.89) | (20.00) | (18.89) | (100.00) |
| Commercial | 1 | 17 | 2 | 2 | 30 |
| | (3.33) | (56.67) | (6.67) | (6.67) | (100.00) |
| Agricultural | 6 | 25 | 7 | 5 | 30 |
| | (20.00) | (83.33) | (23.33) | (16.67) | (100.00) |
| Small Power | 3 | 20 | 13 | 9 | 30 |
| | (10.00) | (66.67) | (43.33) | (30.00) | (100.00) |
| Medium Power | 2 | 22 | 6 | 6 | 30 |
| | (6.67) | (73.33) | (20.00) | (20.00) | (100.00) |
| Large Power | 1 | 14 | 7 | 5 | 30 |
| | (3.33) | (46.67) | (23.33) | (16.67) | (100.00) |
| Bulk Supply | 1 | 2 | 2 | 1 | 6 |
| | (16.67) | (33.33) | (33.33) | (16.67) | (100.00) |
| Street Lighting | 0 | 0 | 2 | 2 | 3 |
| | (0.00) | (0.00) | (66.67) | (66.67) | (100.00) |
| Total | 28 | 153 | 57 | 47 | 249 |
| | (11.24) | (61.45) | (22.89) | (18.88) | (100.00) |

*Note*: Figures in parentheses show percentages.
*Source*: Field Survey.

desire to conserve energy needs to be inculcated among the consumers, i.e. the consumers need to be sensitized about the private and social costs and benefits of avoiding the wastage of power.

Table 4.6 shows the reasons for the people's indulgence in the theft of power as perceived by consumers. The most important reason turned out to be to save money by escaping having to pay for consumption of electricity. The general thinking was: why not do it when it is conveniently possible. This rationale was cited by 84 per cent of respondent consumers, that included 89 per cent of domestic consumers, 90 per cent of commercial consumers, 73 per cent of agricultural consumers, 97 per cent of small power consumers, 70 per cent of medium power consumers, 83 per cent of large power consumers, and 67 per cent each of consumers of bulk supply and street lights. This was followed by high rates of tariff (41 per cent) and inadequate

TABLE 4.5: WAYS IN WHICH CONSUMERS WASTE POWER (KNOWLEDGE OF ENERGY CONSERVATION MEASURES)

| Category of Consumers | Unnecessary use of Electricity | Use of Appliances of Higher Wattage than is Required | Lack of Knowledge of Energy-Efficient Appliances | Ostentatious use during Ceremonies | Any Other | Total Respondents |
|---|---|---|---|---|---|---|
| Domestic | 79 (87.78) | 48 (53.33) | 17 (18.89) | 11 (12.22) | 3 (3.33) | 90 (100.00) |
| Commercial | 27 (90.00) | 15 (50.00) | 0 (0.00) | 5 (16.67) | 1 (3.33) | 30 (100.00) |
| Agricultural | 27 (90.00) | 16 (53.33) | 1 (3.33) | 2 (6.67) | 3 (10.00) | 30 (100.00) |
| Small Power | 29 (96.67) | 12 (40.00) | 3 (10.00) | 2 (6.67) | 1 (3.33) | 30 (100.00) |
| Medium Power | 28 (93.33) | 13 (43.33) | 5 (16.67) | 2 (6.67) | 1 (3.33) | 30 (100.00) |
| Large Power | 28 (93.33) | 14 (46.67) | 3 (10.00) | 3 (10.00) | 1 (3.33) | 30 (100.00) |
| Bulk Supply | 6 (100.00) | 2 (33.33) | 0 (0.00) | 0 (0.00) | 0 (0.00) | 6 (100.00) |
| Street Lighting | 3 (100.00) | 1 (33.33) | 0 (0.00) | 0 (0.00) | 0 (0.00) | 3 (100.00) |
| Total | 227 (91.16) | 121 (48.59) | 29 (11.65) | 25 (10.04) | 10 (4.02) | 249 (100.00) |

*Note*: Figures in parentheses show percentages.
*Source*: Field Survey.

TABLE 4.6: REASONS FOR THEFT OF POWER BY CONSUMERS

| Category of Consumer | Inadequate Supply | Saving of Money | High Rates of Tariff | Legal Connection Difficult | Habitual Pratice | Don't Know | Total Respondents |
|---|---|---|---|---|---|---|---|
| Domestic | 24 | 80 | 40 | 3 | 1 | 0 | 90 |
| | (26.67) | (88.89) | (44.44) | (3.33) | (1.11) | (0.00) | (100.00) |
| Commercial | 7 | 27 | 13 | 0 | 1 | 0 | 30 |
| | (23.33) | (90.00) | (43.33) | (0.00) | (3.33) | (0.00) | (100.00) |
| Agricultural | 11 | 22 | 13 | 0 | 1 | 1 | 30 |
| | (36.67) | (73.33) | (43.33) | (0.00) | (3.33) | (3.33) | (100.00) |
| Small Power | 11 | 29 | 7 | 0 | 1 | 0 | 30 |
| | (36.67) | (96.67) | (23.33) | (0.00) | (3.33) | (0.00) | (100.00) |
| Medium Power | 9 | 21 | 11 | 0 | 2 | 1 | 30 |
| | (30.00) | (70.00) | (36.67) | (0.00) | (6.67) | (3.33) | (100.00) |
| Large Power | 5 | 25 | 13 | 0 | 1 | 1 | 30 |
| | (16.67) | (83.33) | (43.33) | (0.00) | (3.33) | (3.33) | (100.00) |
| Bulkk Supply | 1 | 4 | 4 | 0 | 0 | 1 | 6 |
| | (16.67) | (66.67) | (66.67) | (0.00) | (0.00) | (16.67) | (100.00) |
| Street Lightning | 2 | 2 | 0 | 0 | 0 | 1 | 3 |
| | (66.67) | (66.67) | 0.00 | (0.00) | (0.00) | (33.33) | (100.00) |
| Total | 70 | 210 | 101 | 3 | 7 | 5 | 249 |
| | (28.11) | (84.34) | (40.56) | (1.20) | (2.81) | (2.01) | (100.00) |

*Note*: Figures in parentheses show percentages.
*Source*: Field Survey.

supply of power (28 per cent). Thus, high rates of tariff, directly or indirectly, emerged as one of the main causes of the theft of power. However, this result needs to be interpreted with caution. People appear to be ignorant of or tend to forget that the electricity being supplied to them is below the actual cost of supply and that the agricultural and domestic consumers are being highly subsidized by the government. So the rates of tariff are in fact low and not high, as people believe them to be.

Consumers were asked during what time of the day was the theft of energy really committed. It is generally believed that power theft takes place at night when there is little checking. In our survey, a large majority (75 per cent) of the consumers said that theft was committed during night time. About 4 per cent of the consumers were of the view that it was committed during day time, and about 21 per cent of them mentioned that it was committed at any time of the day. However, the consumers seemed to be divided as to the season in which theft was most frequently committed. Nearly one-half of the consumers expressed the opinion that theft was committed throughout the year. About 42 per cent of the consumers were of the view that it was committed most often during the summer season. Only a small percentage of consumers (7 per cent) mentioned that it was committed during the winter season.

Consumers were asked as to which category of consumers indulged in more pilferage of power than others. A large majority of consumers (87 per cent) believed that industrial consumers indulged in pilferage more than the other categories of consumers. Only 8 per cent of the consumers mentioned that domestic consumers indulged in the theft of power more than the other categories.

The consumers were asked about the social, educational, economic, and political background of the people indulging in the theft of power. As far as social, educational, and economic backgrounds are concerned, a large majority of consumers (more than 70 per cent) mentioned that people of various social backgrounds, both educated and uneducated and both rich and poor, were involved in the pilferage of power. As to the political background, a majority of the consumers (57 per cent) were of the view that the people who indulged in the theft of power were politically influential, i.e. they enjoyed the patronage of higher officials and/or local politicians.

The perception of consumers regarding the involvement of the employees in the theft of power is presented in Table 4.7. The fact that power theft is not possible without the connivance of employees was brought out by a very large majority of consumers (89 per cent). About 7 per cent of the consumers denied the involvement of employees in the theft of power. Only 4 per cent of the consumers expressed ignorance about the involvement of employees.

The extent of involvement of employees in the theft of power is presented in Table 4.8. A majority of consumers (52 per cent) were of the opinion that the involvement of the employees was to a small extent. However, 36 per cent of the consumers mentioned that employees were involved to a large extent. About 5 per cent of the consumers did not know the extent of involvement of the employees.

When asked about the level of involvement of employees in the theft of power, the opinion of the consumers was found to be divided. As is clear from Table 4.9, a little less than one-half of the consumers (48 per cent) were of the view that only lower-level employees (such as meter readers, linemen, etc.) were involved. About 18 per cent

TABLE 4.7: INVOLVEMENT OF EMPLOYEES IN THEFT OF POWER

| Category of Consumers | Involved | Not Involved | Don't Know | Total Respondents |
|---|---|---|---|---|
| Domestic | 78 | 8 | 4 | 90 |
| | (86.67) | (8.89) | (4.44) | (100.00) |
| Commercial | 28 | 1 | 1 | 30 |
| | (93.33) | (3.33) | (3.33) | (100.00) |
| Agricultural | 28 | 2 | 0 | 30 |
| | (93.33) | (6.67) | (0.00) | (100.00) |
| Small Power | 26 | 3 | 1 | 30 |
| | (86.67) | (10.00) | (3.33) | (100.00) |
| Medium Power | 26 | 3 | 1 | 30 |
| | (86.67) | (10.00) | (3.33) | (100.00) |
| Large Power | 27 | 3 | 3 | 33 |
| | (81.82) | (9.09) | (9.09) | (100.00) |
| Bulk Supply | 5 | 0 | 1 | 6 |
| | (83.33) | (0.00) | (16.67) | (100.00) |
| Street Lighting | 3 | 0 | 0 | 3 |
| | (100.00) | (0.00) | (0.00) | (100.00) |
| Total | 221 | 17 | 11 | 249 |
| | (88.76) | (6.83) | (4.42) | (100.00) |

*Note*: Figures in parentheses show percentages.
*Source*: Field Survey.

TABLE 4.8: EXTENT OF INVOLVEMENT OF EMPLOYEES IN THEFT OF POWER

| Category of consumer | Large | Small | No Involvement | Don't Know/No Comments | Total Respondents |
|---|---|---|---|---|---|
| Domestic | 31 (34.44) | 49 (54.44) | 6 (6.67) | 4 (4.44) | 90 (100.00) |
| Commercial | 14 (46.67) | 14 (46.67) | 1 (3.33) | 1 (3.33) | 30 (100.00) |
| Agricultural | 11 (36.67) | 17 (56.67) | 2 (6.67) | 0 (0.00) | 30 (100.00) |
| Small Power | 7 (23.33) | 18 (60.00) | 4 (13.33) | 1 (3.33) | 30 (100.00) |
| Medium Power | 12 (40.00) | 14 (46.67) | 3 (10.00) | 1 (3.33) | 30 (100.00) |
| Large Power | 13 (43.33) | 13 (43.33) | 0 (0.00) | 4 (13.33) | 30 (100.00) |
| Bulk Supply | 2 (33.33) | 2 (33.33) | 1 (16.67) | 1 (16.67) | 6 (100.00) |
| Street lighting | 1 (33.33) | 2 (66.67) | 0 (0.00) | 0 (0.00) | 3 (100.00) |
| Total | 91 (36.55) | 129 (51.81) | 17 (6.83) | 12 (4.82) | 249 (100.00) |

*Note*: Figures in parentheses show percentages.
*Source*: Field Survey.

of them felt that only higher-level employees (JEs onwards) were involved. About 21 per cent of them mentioned that all levels of employees were involved in the theft of power.

As regards the nature of mutually beneficial contracts (bribes, payment of money, etc.) between the employees and the consumers (Table 4.10), a majority of consumers (63 per cent) held the view that such deals between employees and consumers were conducted both in cash and kind. For 12 per cent of the consumers, it involved either cash or kind. About 6 per cent of the consumers did not know any thing about the nature of these contracts.

It was generally believed by the respondent consumers that the employees who connive in power theft enjoyed the backing of higher officials and/or local politicians. Table 4.11 shows that 44 per cent of the consumers mentioned that these employees enjoyed the backing/protection of both higher officials and local politicians. About 17 per cent of the consumers believed that the employees had the

TABLE 4.9: OFFICIAL LEVEL OF EMPLOYEES INVOLVED IN THEFT OF POWER

| Category of Consumer | Higher Officials (JE & Above) | Lower Officials (Below JE) | All are Involved | No Involvement | Don't Know/ No Comments | Total Respondents |
|---|---|---|---|---|---|---|
| Domestic | 15 | 48 | 17 | 6 | 4 | 90 |
| | (16.67) | (53.33) | (18.89) | (6.67) | (4.44) | (100.00) |
| Commercial | 8 | 14 | 6 | 0 | 2 | 30 |
| | (26.67) | (46.67) | (20.00) | (0.00) | (6.67) | (100.00) |
| Agricultural | 10 | 12 | 5 | 3 | 0 | 30 |
| | (33.33) | (40.00) | (16.67) | (10.00) | (0.00) | (100.00) |
| Small Power | 1 | 16 | 9 | 2 | 2 | 30 |
| | (3.33) | (53.33) | (30.00) | (6.67) | (6.67) | (100.00) |
| Medium Power | 2 | 13 | 9 | 5 | 1 | 30 |
| | (6.67) | (43.33) | (30.00) | (16.67) | (3.33) | (100.00) |
| Large Power | 7 | 12 | 6 | 1 | 4 | 30 |
| | (23.33) | (40.00) | (20.00) | (3.33) | (13.33) | (100.00) |
| Bulk Supply | 1 | 3 | 1 | 0 | 1 | 6 |
| | (16.67) | (50.00) | (16.67) | (0.00) | (16.67) | (100.00) |
| Street lighting | 1 | 2 | 0 | 0 | 0 | 3 |
| | (33.33) | (66.67) | (0.00) | (0.00) | (0.00) | (100.00) |
| Total | 45 | 120 | 53 | 17 | 14 | 249 |
| | (18.07) | (48.19) | (21.29) | (6.83) | (5.62) | (100.00) |

*Note*: Figures in parentheses show percentages.
*Source*: Field Survey.

TABLE 4.10: NATURE OF BENEFICIAL CONTRACTS (BRIBES, ETC.) BETWEEN EMPLOYEES AND CONSUMERS

| Category of Consumer | Cash | Kind | Both Cash & Kind | No Involvement | Don't Know/ No Comments | Total Respondents |
|---|---|---|---|---|---|---|
| Domestic | 11 | 8 | 61 | 6 | 4 | 90 |
| | (12.22) | (8.89) | (67.78) | (6.67) | (4.44) | (100.00) |
| Commercial | 5 | 5 | 16 | 3 | 1 | 30 |
| | (16.67) | (16.67) | (53.33) | (10.00) | (3.33) | (100.00) |
| Agricultural | 5 | 4 | 18 | 3 | 0 | 30 |
| | (16.67) | (13.33) | (60.00) | (10.00) | 0.00 | (100.00) |
| Small Power | 4 | 4 | 18 | 1 | 3 | 30 |
| | (13.33) | (13.33) | (60.00) | (3.33) | (10.00) | (100.00) |
| Medium Power | 1 | 6 | 20 | 2 | 1 | 30 |
| | (3.33) | (20.00) | (66.67) | (6.67) | (3.33) | (100.00) |
| Large Power | 3 | 2 | 20 | 1 | 4 | 30 |
| | (10.00) | (6.67) | (66.67) | (3.33) | (13.33) | (100.00) |
| Bulk Supply | 1 | 1 | 3 | 0 | 1 | 6 |
| | (16.67) | (16.67) | (50.00) | (0.00) | (16.67) | (100.00) |
| Street Lighting | 0 | 0 | 2 | 1 | 0 | 3 |
| | (0.00) | (0.00) | (66.67) | (33.33) | (0.00) | (100.00) |
| Total | 30 | 30 | 158 | 17 | 14 | 249 |
| | (12.05) | (12.05) | (63.45) | (6.83) | (5.62) | (100.00) |

*Note*: Figures in parentheses show percentages.
*Source*: Field Survey.

TABLE 4.11: BACKING/PROTECTION ENJOYED BY THE EMPLOYEES INVOLVED IN THEFT OF POWER

| Category of Consumer | Local Politicians | Higher Officials | Both Local Politicians & Higher Officials | No Backing | No Comments | Total Respondents |
|---|---|---|---|---|---|---|
| Domestic | 7 (7.78) | 21 (23.33) | 37 (41.11) | 20 (22.22) | 5 (5.56) | 90 (100.00) |
| Commercial | 4 (13.33) | 7 (23.33) | 15 (50.00) | 2 (6.67) | 2 (6.67) | 30 (100.00) |
| Agricultural | 1 (3.33) | 6 (20.00) | 19 (63.33) | 4 (13.33) | 0 (0.00) | 30 (100.00) |
| Small Power | 5 (16.67) | 3 (10.00) | 11 (36.67) | 9 (30.00) | 2 (6.67) | 30 (100.00) |
| Medium Power | 2 (6.67) | 2 (6.67) | 9 (30.00) | 13 (43.33) | 4 (13.33) | 30 (100.00) |
| Large Power | 1 (3.33) | 3 (10.00) | 15 (50.00) | 6 (20.00) | 5 (16.67) | 30 (100.00) |
| Bulk Supply | 0 (0.00) | 1 (16.67) | 3 (50.00) | 1 (16.67) | 1 (16.67) | 6 (100.00) |
| Street lighting | 1 (33.33) | 0 (0.00) | 1 (33.33) | 1 (33.33) | 0 (0.00) | 3 (100.00) |
| Total | 21 (8.43) | 43 (17.27) | 110 (44.18) | 56 (22.49) | 19 (7.63) | 249 (100.00) |

*Note*: Figures in parentheses show percentages.
*Source*: Field Survey.

protection of higher officials, and 8 per cent of them claimed that local politicians protected them. However, 22 per cent of consumers felt that the employees had no backing and operated on their own.

### 2. *Methods used to Pilfer Power and the Methods to Check it*

There are a number of methods which may be employed by unscrupulous consumers pilfer power, such as tampering of meters, use of *kundies*/direct supply from distribution lines, use of defective meters, etc. Our enquiries from consumers revealed that a majority of them (52 per cent) shared the view that all these methods were used by consumers (Table 4.12). The use of *kundies*/direct supply from distribution lines was mentioned by 33 per cent of the consumers. Tampering of meters was mentioned by about 30 per cent of the consumers, and about 7 per cent of the consumers mentioned defective/damaging meters as the method of committing theft of power. Only 2 per cent of the consumers mentioned other methods, and 2 per cent respondents expressed ignorance about the methods employed by different categories of consumers.

As far as effective methods of checking pilferage of power are concerned, we have grouped the perceptions of consumers under five broad headings:

1. Technical methods: Methods such as improving the sealing systems, the immediate replacement of burnt out or defective meters, etc.
2. Organizational methods: Changes in the organization of the State Electricity Board to make administration more accountable, effective, and responsive.
3. Social Methods: Creating social awareness among people regarding the ill effects of power theft, exposing unscrupulous consumers before the public, involvement of NGOs, involving panchayats, and municipal committees, etc.
4. Changes in the tariff structure, i.e. increasing or decreasing the tariff rates for various categories of consumers.
5. Checking by the field staff as well as by the enforcement staff.

Table 4.13 shows the details of the technical methods used to check the pilferage of power. The most effective method suggested by a majority of consumers (60 per cent) was the improvement in the sealing system of the meters. This also included tamper-proof sealing

TABLE 4.12: METHODS EMPLOYED BY DIFFERENT CATEGORIES OF CONSUMERS FOR THEFT OF POWER

| Category of Consumer | Tampering with Meters | Defective Meters | Use of *Kundies*/ Direct Supply From Lines | All of These | Any Other | Don't Know | Total Respondents |
|---|---|---|---|---|---|---|---|
| Domestic | 27 | 9 | 31 | 46 | 3 | 3 | 90 |
| | (30.00) | (10.00) | (34.44) | (51.11) | (3.33) | (3.33) | (100.00) |
| Commercial | 7 | 0 | 9 | 19 | 0 | 0 | 30 |
| | (23.33) | 0.00 | (30.00) | (63.33) | (0.00) | (0.00) | (100.00) |
| Agricultural | 9 | 5 | 7 | 15 | 1 | 0 | 30 |
| | (30.00) | (16.67) | (23.33) | (50.00) | (3.33) | (0.00) | (100.00) |
| Small Power | 15 | 1 | 14 | 10 | 0 | 0 | 30 |
| | (50.00) | (3.33) | (46.67) | (33.33) | (0.00) | (0.00) | (100.00) |
| Medium Power | 7 | 2 | 10 | 16 | 0 | 1 | 30 |
| | (23.33) | (6.67) | (33.33) | (53.33) | (0.00) | (3.33) | (100.00) |
| Large Power | 10 | 0 | 9 | 16 | 1 | 2 | 30 |
| | (33.33) | (0.00) | (30.00) | (53.33) | (3.33) | (6.67) | (100.00) |
| Bulk Supply | 1 | 0 | 1 | 5 | 0 | 0 | 6 |
| | (16.67) | (0.00) | (16.67) | (83.33) | (0.00) | (0.00) | (100.00) |
| Street Lighting | 0 | 0 | 1 | 2 | 0 | 0 | 3 |
| | (0.00) | (0.00) | (33.33) | (66.67) | (0.00) | (0.00) | (100.00) |
| Total | 76 | 17 | 82 | 129 | 5 | 6 | 249 |
| | (30.52) | (6.83) | (32.93) | (51.81) | (2.01) | (2.41) | (100.00) |

*Note*: Figures in parentheses show percentages.
*Source*: Field Survey.

TABLE 4.13: TECHNICAL METHODS OF CONTAINING THEFT OF POWER

| Category of Consumer | Improve Sealing System of Meters/ Joints | Replace Burnt/ Defective Meters Immediately | Install Meters at one Point in Village/ Locality | All of These | Total Respon- dents |
|---|---|---|---|---|---|
| Domestic | 60 | 39 | 31 | 7 | 90 |
| | (66.67) | (43.33) | (34.44) | (7.78) | (100.00) |
| Commercial | 18 | 12 | 12 | 4 | 30 |
| | (60.00) | (40.00) | (40.00) | (13.33) | (100.00) |
| Agricultural | 16 | 16 | 9 | 3 | 30 |
| | (53.33) | (53.33) | (30.00) | (10.00) | (100.00) |
| Small Power | 18 | 10 | 18 | 1 | 30 |
| | (60.00) | (33.33) | (60.00) | (3.33) | (100.00) |
| Medium Power | 14 | 10 | 16 | 5 | 30 |
| | (46.67) | (33.33) | (53.33) | (16.67) | (100.00) |
| Large Power | 19 | 11 | 8 | 3 | 30 |
| | (63.33) | (36.67) | (26.67) | (10.00) | (100.00) |
| Bulk Supply | 3 | 2 | 5 | 0 | 6 |
| | (50.00) | (33.33) | (83.33) | (0.00) | (100.00) |
| Street Lighting | 2 | 1 | 1 | 0 | 3 |
| | (66.67) | (33.33) | (33.33) | (0.00) | (100.00) |
| Total | 150 | 101 | 100 | 23 | 249 |
| | (60.24) | (40.56) | (40.16) | (9.24) | (100.00) |

*Note*: Figures in parentheses show percentages.
*Source*: Field Survey.

of all joints. Other methods suggested were replacing burnt out/ defective meters immediately (40 per cent) and installing meters and distribution transformers at one point in a village/locality (40 per cent).

Table 4.14 depicts the organizational methods to contain power theft. A majority of consumers (51 per cent) suggested that the responsibility of each employee should be clearly demarcated and fixed. About 48 per cent of them suggested that there should be a regular transfer of the field staff so as to break the nexus between them and the consumers. In fact, one of the ex-members of the PSEB whom the study team met in Amritsar pointed out that it was the only method of checking power theft in Punjab. About 29 per cent of consumers suggested that incentives should be provided to employees to motivate them towards their duty. And about one-fifth of the consumers

TABLE 4.14: ORGANIZATIONAL METHODS OF CONTAINING THEFT OF POWER

| Category of Consumers | Responsibility of each Employee be Fixed | Regular Transfer of Employees | Incentive Should be Provided | Punishment Should be made Stringent | Involve Employees' Union | Any Other | Total Respondents |
|---|---|---|---|---|---|---|---|
| Domestic | 45 | 39 | 25 | 20 | 6 | 0 | 90 |
| | (50.00) | (43.33) | (27.78) | (22.22) | (6.67) | (0.00) | (100.00) |
| Commercial | 14 | 14 | 10 | 4 | 1 | 1 | 30 |
| | (46.67) | (46.67) | (33.33) | (13.33) | (3.33) | (3.33) | (100.00) |
| Agricultural | 19 | 13 | 9 | 6 | 2 | 1 | 30 |
| | (63.33) | (43.33) | (30.00) | (20.00) | (6.67) | (3.33) | (100.00) |
| Small Power | 16 | 16 | 10 | 5 | 11 | 1 | 30 |
| | (53.33) | (53.33) | (33.33) | (16.67) | (36.67) | (3.33) | (100.00) |
| Medium Power | 12 | 17 | 7 | 6 | 1 | 2 | 30 |
| | (40.00) | (56.67) | (23.33) | (20.00) | (3.33) | (6.67) | (100.00) |
| Large Power | 16 | 15 | 9 | 4 | 1 | 1 | 30 |
| | (53.33) | (50.00) | (30.00) | (13.33) | (3.33) | (3.33) | (100.00) |
| Bulk Supply | 3 | 4 | 1 | 1 | 1 | 0 | 6 |
| | (50.00) | (66.67) | (16.67) | (16.67) | (16.67) | (0.00) | (100.00) |
| Street Lighting | 2 | 1 | 1 | 1 | 0 | 0 | 3 |
| | (66.67) | (33.33) | (33.33) | (33.33) | (0.00) | (0.00) | (100.00) |
| Total | 127 | 119 | 72 | 47 | 13 | 6 | 249 |
| | (51.00) | (47.79) | (28.92) | (18.88) | (5.22) | (2.41) | (100.00) |

*Note*: Figures in parentheses show percentages.
*Source*: Field Survey.

suggested stringent punishment for those indulging in the theft of power.

As regards the social methods of checking the theft of power (Table 4.15), a majority of consumers (60 per cent) suggested both increasing social awareness and exposing unscrupulous consumers before the public as the most effective methods.

Table 4.16 deals with the various methods relating to changes in the tariff structure. As has already been pointed out, the high rate of tariff was found to be an important reason for the theft of power. About one-half of the consumers felt that tariffs were on the higher side and suggested that they should be reduced. However, 26 per cent of the consumers suggested that tariff rates were reasonable but emphasized the need to improve the quality of service provied to the consumers.

TABLE 4.15: SOCIAL METHODS OF CONTAINING THEFT OF POWER

| Category of Consumer | Social Awareness Among People | Expose People in Public | Both Social Public Exposure | Don't Know/ No Comments | Total Respondents |
|---|---|---|---|---|---|
| Domestic | 20 | 20 | 52 | 4 | 90 |
| | (22.22) | (22.22) | (57.78) | (4.44) | (100.00) |
| Commercial | 7 | 8 | 18 | 2 | 30 |
| | (23.33) | (26.67) | (60.00) | (6.67) | (100.00) |
| Agricultural | 5 | 10 | 17 | 1 | 30 |
| | (16.67) | (33.33) | (56.67) | (3.33) | (100.00) |
| Small Power | 4 | 2 | 24 | 1 | 30 |
| | (13.33) | (6.67) | (80.00) | (3.33) | (100.00) |
| Medium Power | 4 | 5 | 15 | 4 | 30 |
| | (13.33) | (16.67) | (50.00) | (13.33) | (100.00) |
| Large Power | 8 | 6 | 17 | 1 | 30 |
| | (26.67) | (20.00) | (56.67) | (3.33) | (100.00) |
| Bulk Supply | 1 | 1 | 5 | 0 | 6 |
| | (16.67) | (16.67) | (83.33) | (0.00) | (100.00) |
| Street Lighting | 1 | 0 | 2 | 0 | 3 |
| | (33.33) | (0.00) | (66.67) | (0.00) | (100.00) |
| Total | 50 | 52 | 150 | 13 | 249 |
| | (20.08) | (20.88) | (60.24) | (5.22) | (100.00) |

*Note*: Figures in parentheses show percentages.
*Source*: Field Survey.

TABLE 4.16: CHANGES IN TARIFF STRUCTURE TO CONTAIN THEFT OF POWER

| Category of Consumer | Monthly Minimum Charges be Increased | Tariff Should be Increased | No Change in Tariff but Quality of Service be Improved | Total Respondents |
|---|---|---|---|---|
| Domestic | 28 (31.11) | 49 (54.44) | 23 (25.56) | 90 (100.00) |
| Commercial | 13 (43.33) | 15 (50.00) | 6 (20.00) | 30 (100.00) |
| Agricultural | 7 (23.33) | 17 (56.67) | 6 (20.00) | 30 (100.00) |
| Small Power | 7 (23.33) | 11 (36.67) | 12 (40.00) | 30 (100.00) |
| Medium Power | 7 (23.33) | 15 (50.00) | 7 (23.33) | 30 (100.00) |
| Large Power | 10 (33.33) | 15 (50.00) | 7 (23.33) | 33 (100.00) |
| Bulk Supply | 2 (33.33) | 2 (33.33) | 2 (33.33) | 6 (100.00) |
| Street Lighting | 1 (33.33) | 0 (0.00) | 2 (66.67) | 3 (100.00) |
| Total | 75 (30.12) | 124 (49.80) | 65 (26.10) | 249 (100.00) |

*Note*: Figures in parentheses show percentages.
*Source*: Field Survey.

Checking both by the field staff and the enforcement staff (flying squad, etc.) plays an important role in detecting the theft of power and in formulating an effective strategy to contain this problem. That is why a majority of consumers (59 per cent) suggested that checking by staff should be both frequent and random (Table 4.17). Another 26 per cent of the consumers suggested random checking, and about 19 per cent of them suggested frequent checking.

The consumers were asked as to what punishment should be given to people guilty of stealing power. The imposition of monetary fines and the disconnection of supply emerged as the main punishments recommended by a majority of consumers (68 per cent and 61 per cent respectively). Only 17 per cent of consumers suggested harsh punishment like imprisonment. A very few consumers (4 per cent) were in favour of publicly exposing the culprits (Table 4.18).

TABLE 4.17: CHECKING BY STAFF TO CONTAIN THEFT OF POWER

| Category of Consumer | Frequent Checking | Random Checking | Both Frequent & Random Checking | Any Other | Don't Know/ No Comments | Total Respondents |
|---|---|---|---|---|---|---|
| Domestic | 15 | 30 | 52 | 6 | 0 | 90 |
| | (16.67) | (33.33) | (57.78) | (6.67) | 0.00 | (100.00) |
| Commercial | 7 | 7 | 15 | 2 | 1 | 30 |
| | (23.33) | (23.33) | (50.00) | (6.67) | (3.33) | (100.00) |
| Agriculutral | 9 | 7 | 18 | 1 | 0 | 30 |
| | (30.00) | (23.33) | (60.00) | (3.33) | (0.00) | (100.00) |
| Small Power | 7 | 8 | 17 | 1 | 0 | 30 |
| | (23.33) | (26.67) | (56.67) | (3.33) | (0.00) | (100.00) |
| Medium Power | 4 | 5 | 18 | 0 | 2 | 30 |
| | (13.33) | (16.67) | (60.00) | (0.00) | (6.67) | (100.00) |
| Large Power | 5 | 8 | 19 | 0 | 1 | 30 |
| | (16.67) | (26.67) | (63.33) | (0.00) | (3.33) | (100.00) |
| Bulk Supply | 0 | 1 | 5 | 0 | 0 | 6 |
| | (0.00) | (16.67) | (83.33) | (0.00) | (0.00) | (100.00) |
| Street Lighting | 0 | 0 | 3 | 0 | 0 | 3 |
| | (0.00) | (0.00) | (100.00) | (0.00) | (0.00) | (0.00) |
| Total | 47 | 66 | 147 | 10 | 4 | 249 |
| | (18.88) | (26.51) | (59.04) | (4.02) | (1.61) | (100.00) |

*Note*: Figures in parentheses show percentages.
*Source*: Field Survey.

### 3. *Perceptions Regarding the Tariff Rates*

The consumers were asked as to how far people came to know about the negative effects of the pilferage of power. It was found that a large majority of them (more than 80 per cent) were aware of the negative effects associated with the pilferage of power such as the fall in the voltage, frequent breakdowns, financial losses to the PSEB and consequently lower levels of new investments, less availability of power in the future, poor quality of service, and breeding of corruption among employees.

Consumers were asked whether there should be a flat rate system or metered supply for agricultural consumers. A majority of consumers (62 per cent) were strongly in favour of metered supply to the agricultural sector, which included 59 per cent of domestic consumers, 60 per cent of commercial consumers, 47 per cent of agricultural consumers, 67 per cent of small power consumers, 63 per cent of medium power consumers, 77 per cent of large power consumers, 83 per cent of bulk supply consumers, and 67 per cent of street lighting. The flat rate system found favour only among agricultural consumers; a majority of them (53 per cent) advocated its continuance. The reasons why the flat rate system was rejected in favour of metered supply by a majority of consumers were:

(i) In this system it is difficult to monitor how much power is consumed by a particular consumer.
(ii) The consumers pay the same amount of money even if their consumption of power may vary.

The consumers were asked whether the different categories of consumers should be charged tariff at the same rate or at different (prices) according to the cost of supply to them. An overwhelming majority (87 per cent) of consumers suggested that there should be different rates. About 12 per cent of them were in favour of the same rates, and 1 per cent did not like to comment on the issue.

### 4. *Efficacy of the Organization and Accountability*

The consumers were asked questions relating to the organizational structure of the PSEB, i.e. whether the present structure should be continued or whether there should be privatization. The privatization of the PSEB was strongly advocated by a large majority of consum-

TABLE 4.18: PUNISHMENT FOR COMMITTING THEFT OF POWER

| Category of Consumer | Monetary Fine | Dis-connection of Supply | Imprison-ment | Expose Through Public Meetings | Expose Through TV/Radio/ Newspapers | All of These | Any Other | Dont't Know | Total Res-pondents |
|---|---|---|---|---|---|---|---|---|---|
| Domestic | 61<br>(67.78) | 60<br>(66.67) | 11<br>(12.22) | 6<br>(6.67) | 1<br>(1.11) | 6<br>(6.67) | 2<br>(2.22) | 0<br>(0.00) | 90<br>(100.00) |
| Commercial | 21<br>(70.00) | 20<br>(66.67) | 8<br>(26.67) | 1<br>(3.33) | 2<br>(6.67) | 0<br>(0.00) | 1<br>(3.33) | 0<br>(0.00) | 30<br>(100.00) |
| Agricultural | 20<br>(66.67) | 16<br>(53.33) | 4<br>(13.33) | 2<br>(6.67) | 1<br>(3.33) | 1<br>(3.33) | 1<br>(3.33) | 1<br>(3.33) | 30<br>(100.00) |
| Small Power | 27<br>(90.00) | 20<br>(66.67) | 7<br>(23.33) | 0<br>(0.00) | 0<br>(0.00) | 0<br>(0.00) | 0<br>(0.00) | 0<br>(0.00) | 30<br>(100.00) |
| Medium Power | 15<br>(50.00) | 10<br>(33.33) | 8<br>(26.67) | 1<br>(3.33) | 1<br>(3.33) | 3<br>(10.00) | 1<br>(3.33) | 2<br>(6.67) | 30<br>(100.00) |
| Large Power | 21<br>(70.00) | 20<br>(66.67) | 3<br>(10.00) | 0<br>(0.00) | 0<br>(0.00) | 1<br>(3.33) | 0<br>(0.00) | 1<br>(3.33) | 30<br>(100.00) |
| Bulk Supply | 3<br>(50.00) | 3<br>(50.00) | 2<br>(33.33) | 0<br>(0.00) | 0<br>(0.00) | 1<br>(16.67) | 0<br>(0.00) | 0<br>(0.00) | 6<br>(100.00) |
| Street Lighting | 2<br>(66.67) | 3<br>(100.00) | 0<br>(0.00) | 0<br>(0.00) | 0<br>(0.00) | 0<br>(0.00) | 1<br>(33.33) | 0<br>(0.00) | 3<br>(100.00) |
| Total | 170<br>(68.27) | 152<br>(61.04) | 43<br>(17.27) | 10<br>(4.02) | 5<br>(2.01) | 12<br>(4.82) | 6<br>(2.41) | 4<br>(1.61) | 249<br>(100.00) |

*Note*: Figures in parentheses show percentages.
*Source*: Field Survey.

ers (72 per cent) who included 59 per cent of domestic consumers, 70 per cent of commercial consumers, 53 per cent of agricultural consumers, 87 per cent of small power consumers, 97 per cent of medium power consumers, 83 per cent of large power consumers, and all the consumers of bulk supply and street lighting. In fact, privatization (of distribution of electricity) was believed to be the panacea for the ills of the PSEB. The reasons advanced for privatization were: (i) It would improve the quality of service to consumers. (ii) It would reduce harassment of consumers. (iii) It would lead to less corruption among employees (Table 4.19).

Although the consumers were aware that privatization would lead to an increase in the price of the service to the consumers, yet a fair number of consumers mentioned that they did not mind paying a higher price if the quality of service was improved. They were also asked whether some category of consumers (especially agricultural) should be subsidized. A large majority of them (66 per cent) were in

TABLE 4.19: PRIVATIZATION OF PSEB

| Category of Consumers | It Should be Privatized | It Should not be Privatized | Don't Known | Total Respondents |
|---|---|---|---|---|
| Domestic | 53<br>(58.89) | 35<br>(38.89) | 2<br>(2.22) | 90<br>(100.00) |
| Commercial | 21<br>(70.00) | 8<br>(26.67) | 1<br>(3.33) | 30<br>(100.00) |
| Agricultural | 16<br>(53.33) | 14<br>(46.67) | 0<br>(0.00) | 30<br>(100.00) |
| Small Power | 26<br>(86.67) | 4<br>(13.33) | 0<br>(0.00) | 30<br>(100.00) |
| Medium Power | 29<br>(96.67) | 1<br>(3.33) | 0<br>(0.00) | 30<br>(100.00) |
| Large Power | 25<br>(83.33) | 5<br>(16.67) | 0<br>(0.00) | 30<br>(100.00) |
| Bulk Supply | 6<br>(100.00) | 0<br>(0.00) | 0<br>(0.00) | 6<br>(100.00) |
| Street Lighting | 3<br>(100.00) | 0<br>(0.00) | 0<br>(0.00) | 3<br>(100.00) |
| Total | 179<br>(71.89) | 67<br>(26.91) | 3<br>(1.20) | 249<br>(100.00) |

*Note*: Figures in parentheses show percentages.
*Source*: Field Survey.

favour of subsidizing the electricity supply for irrigation even after privatization.

The consumers were asked as to what steps should be taken to improve the accountability of employees towards their duty.

Table 4.20 gives the details of their responses. The most important step suggested by a large majority of consumers (77 per cent) was the enforcement of strict supervision over the employees so that no dereliction of duty occurred on their part. About 57 per cent of the consumers wanted responsibility of each category of employees to be clearly demarcated and fixed. About 14 per cent of consumers suggested other methods, such as providing more incentives, improved

TABLE 4.20: STEPS TO IMPROVE ACCOUNTABILITY OF EMPLOYEES TOWARDS THEIR DUTY

| Category of Consumers | Strict Supervision be Enforced | Responsibility of Each Category of Employee be Clearly Demarcated/ Fixed | Any Other (Incentives, Facilities, etc.) | Total Respondents |
|---|---|---|---|---|
| Domestic | 63<br>(70.00) | 51<br>(56.67) | 19<br>(21.11) | 90<br>(100.00) |
| Commercial | 23<br>(76.67) | 18<br>(60.00) | 1<br>(3.33) | 30<br>(100.00) |
| Agricultural | 28<br>(93.33) | 17<br>(56.67) | 0<br>(0.00) | 30<br>(100.00) |
| Small Power | 22<br>(73.33) | 17<br>(56.67) | 7<br>(23.33) | 30<br>(100.00) |
| Medium Power | 23<br>(76.67) | 18<br>(60.00) | 4<br>(13.33) | 30<br>(100.00) |
| Large Power | 26<br>(86.67) | 17<br>(56.67) | 4<br>(13.33) | 30<br>(100.00) |
| Bulk Supply | 4<br>(66.67) | 3<br>(50.00) | 2<br>(33.33) | 6<br>(100.00) |
| Street Lighting | 3<br>(100.00) | 2<br>(66.67) | 0<br>(0.00) | 3<br>(100.00) |
| Total | 192<br>(77.11) | 143<br>(57.43) | 37<br>(14.86) | 249<br>(100.00) |

*Note*: Figures in parentheses show percentages.
*Source*: Field Survey

facilities, better equipments, etc. to the employees so that they discharged their duties more efficiently.

### 5. *Community-based Intervention Strategies*

The consumers were asked whether community-based organizations like gram panchayats or municipal committees should be involved in the distribution of power to check pilferage. A large majority of consumers (68 per cent) were found to be sceptical about the efficacy of involving these organizations in the distribution of power. According to them, these organizations have been highly politicized and their involvement would result in the politicizing of distribution, which would aggravate the already dismal distribution situation. About 29 per cent of the consumers, however, favoured their involvement, and 3 per cent of consumers did not like to comment on the matter. Similarly, an overwhelming majority of consumers was against the involvement of other social organizations/groups such as Rotary Clubs, Gymkhana Clubs, youth clubs, mahila mandals, etc., in the distribution of power. Only 16 per cent of the consumers favoured the involvement of these organizations/groups, of which 6 per cent favoured Rotary Clubs, 5 per cent chose the youth clubs, 3 per cent opted for Gymkhana Clubs, and 2 per cent favoured mahila mandals.

Consumers were asked whether there should be publicity/propaganda (slogans) against the evil of power theft so that people would be discouraged from indulging in this evil practice. A very large number of them (86 per cent) mentioned that there should be publicity (slogans) against the evil of power theft through TV/radio, press, posters, etc. About 6 per cent of them were not enthusiastic about any kind of slogans and argued that nothing would be gained by adopting them. About 8 per cent of the consumers did not know/like to comment on the matter.

The communication strategy for containing power theft involves educating consumers about the negative effects of power theft through various channels such as public meetings, press, TV/radio programmes, street plays, songs, etc. In our survey, consumers were asked to identify the effective ways of communicating with consumers.

Public meetings (73 per cent) and TV/radio programmes (59 per cent) emerged as the most effective ways of communicating with the consumers (Table 4.21). Consumers chose public meetings because this avenue of communication permitted a direct exchange of views

TABLE 4.21: EFFECTIVE WAYS OF COMMUNICATING WITH CONSUMERS

| Category of Consumer | Public Meetings | Ads in the Print Media | TV/Radio Programmes | Street Plays | Songs | All of These | Total Respondents |
|---|---|---|---|---|---|---|---|
| Domestic | 60 | 28 | 53 | 32 | 5 | 17 | 90 |
| | (66.67) | (31.11) | (58.89) | (35.56) | (5.56) | (18.89) | (100.00) |
| Commercial | 26 | 9 | 17 | 11 | 1 | 3 | 30 |
| | (86.67) | (30.00) | (56.67) | (36.67) | (3.33) | (10.00) | (100.00) |
| Agricultural | 24 | 16 | 15 | 9 | 2 | 2 | 30 |
| | (80.00) | (53.33) | (50.00) | (30.00) | (6.67) | (6.67) | (100.00) |
| Small Power | 19 | 10 | 20 | 10 | 4 | 4 | 30 |
| | (63.33) | (33.33) | (66.67) | (33.33) | (13.33) | (13.33) | (100.00) |
| Medium Power | 20 | 10 | 17 | 8 | 4 | 4 | 30 |
| | (66.67) | (33.33) | (56.67) | (26.67) | (13.33) | (13.33) | (100.00) |
| Large Power | 26 | 8 | 18 | 7 | 5 | 2 | 30 |
| | (86.67) | (26.67) | (60.00) | (23.33) | (16.67) | (6.67) | (100.00) |
| Bulk Supply | 5 | 4 | 4 | 2 | 1 | 0 | 6 |
| | (83.33) | (66.67) | (66.67) | (33.33) | (16.67) | (0.00) | (100.00) |
| Street Lighting | 3 | 0 | 2 | 2 | 0 | 0 | 3 |
| | (100.00) | (0.00) | (66.67) | (66.67) | (0.00) | (0.00) | (100.00) |
| Total | 183 | 85 | 146 | 81 | 22 | 32 | 249 |
| | (73.49) | (34.14) | (58.63) | (32.53) | (8.84) | (12.85) | (100.00) |

*Note*: Figures in parentheses show percentages.
*Source*: Field Survey.

between the consumers and the officials of the PSEB, which would thus inculcate a sense of participation in the decision-making process and encourage a sense of moral responsibility to abide by the decisions taken. TV/radio programmes were chosen because of their increasing popularity among people both in the rural and urban areas. The other relatively less important ways of communicating with people mentioned were: advertisements in the press (34 per cent), street plays (32.5 per cent), and songs (9 per cent).

Consumers were asked whether power theft was good or bad. Nearly all of them (98 per cent) felt that it was bad. As to what was bad about it, an overwhelming majority (86 per cent) of them gave two reasons: (i) power theft leads to inferior quality of service to the consumers, and (ii) it leads to financial losses to the PSEB, whereby it cannot make further investments to improve the quality of service (Table 4.22).

Finally, the consumers were asked what steps should be taken to increase their satisfaction. Various steps were suggested by them in this regard (Table 4.23). The most important step suggested by a vast majority of consumers (79 per cent) was that there should be adequate uninterrupted supply of power. The next important step, suggested by 57 per cent of consumers, was the quick redressal of complaints/grievances. About one-half of the consumers suggested a reduction in the tariff rates. The other steps suggested were: periodic meetings with higher officials of the PSEB (28 per cent) and a reduction in voltage fluctuations (14 per cent).

### 6. *Perceptions of Farmers Regarding Misuse of Tube Well Connections*

Agriculture occupies an important place in the Punjab economy. The agricultural sector is the major consumer of electricity. The sectoral break-up of the sale of energy for the year 1998–9 shows that it accounted for more than 35 per cent of the total energy sold within the state. For the agricultural sector in Punjab electricity has been supplied free since 1997–8. Before that, there was a flat rate per horse power (HP) tariff system. This survey was conducted before the agricultural supply was made free of cost and the flat rate system was in operation.

A total number of 30 farmers were interviewed, selecting 10 from each region. They were asked various questions relating to tube well connections. When asked whether generally larger motors (of higher

TABLE 4.22: WHAT IS GOOD OR BAD ABOUT THEFT OF POWER

| Category of Consumers | It Leads to Overloading Whereby the Quality of Service Declines | Financial Loss to PSEB Whereby it cannot invest to Improve the Quality of Service | Power Theft is not Bad—State should otherwise Supply Power Free of Cost | Total Respondents |
|---|---|---|---|---|
| Domestic | 75<br>(83.33) | 75<br>(83.33) | 3<br>(3.33) | 90<br>(100.00) |
| Commercial | 26<br>(86.67) | 29<br>(96.67) | 0<br>(0.00) | 30<br>(100.00) |
| Agricultural | 26<br>(86.67) | 29<br>(96.67) | 0<br>(0.00) | 30<br>(100.00) |
| Small Power | 29<br>(96.67) | 22<br>(73.33) | 0<br>(0.00) | 30<br>(100.00) |
| Medium Power | 29<br>(96.67) | 26<br>(86.67) | 0<br>(0.00) | 30<br>(100.00) |
| Large Power | 23<br>(76.67) | 25<br>(83.33) | 1<br>(3.33) | 30<br>(100.00) |
| Bulk Supply | 4<br>(66.67) | 5<br>(83.33) | 0<br>(0.00) | 6<br>(100.00) |
| Street Lighting | 3<br>(100.00) | 3<br>(100.00) | 0<br>(0.00) | 3<br>(100.00) |
| Total | 215<br>(86.35) | 214<br>(85.94) | 4<br>(1.61) | 249<br>(100.00) |

*Note*: Figures in parentheses show percentages.
*Source*: Field Survey.

BHP) were installed than the sanctioned load, 25 out of 30 consumers, i.e. 83 per cent, replied that farmers mostly resorted to this practice. They do this because during summer time, due to the depletion of underground water, the water level in the tube wells goes down (falling of the water table). In such as situation, a bigger motor (of higher BHP) is required to pump out water from the tube wells.

Farmers were asked questions regarding the use of other electric machines/implements which were powered along with the tube well from the same connection. 11 of them (37 per cent) admitted to using threshers, while 2 of them (7 per cent) mentioned that other machines/implements were used. The use of all types of machines/implements such as threshers, *tokas*, fodder cutters, *atta chakkis*, etc., was admitted by 17 of them (57 per cent).

TABLE 4.23: STEPS TO BE TAKEN TO INCREASE CONSUMERS' SATISFACTION

| Category of Consumer | Adequate Uninterrupted Power Supply | Quick Redressal of Complaints/ Grievances | Tariff Rates Should be Reduced | Periodic Meetings with higher Officials of PSEB | Voltage Fluctuations should be Corrected | Any Other | Total Respondents |
|---|---|---|---|---|---|---|---|
| Domestic | 78<br>(86.67) | 50<br>(55.56) | 59<br>(65.56) | 29<br>(32.22) | 14<br>(15.56) | 1<br>(1.11) | 90<br>(100.00) |
| Commercial | 20<br>(66.67) | 21<br>(70.00) | 15<br>(50.00) | 11<br>(36.67) | 6<br>(20.00) | 1<br>(3.33) | 30<br>(100.00) |
| Agricultural | 17<br>(56.67) | 15<br>(50.00) | 6<br>(20.00) | 6<br>(20.00) | 6<br>(20.00) | 1<br>(3.33) | 30<br>(100.00) |
| Small Power | 29<br>(96.67) | 20<br>(66.67) | 12<br>(40.00) | 6<br>(20.00) | 4<br>(13.33) | 1<br>(3.33) | 30<br>(100.00) |
| Medium Power | 24<br>(80.00) | 11<br>(36.67) | 13<br>(43.33) | 5<br>(16.67) | 4<br>(13.33) | 2<br>(6.67) | 30<br>(100.00) |
| Large Power | 22<br>(73.33) | 20<br>(66.67) | 13<br>(43.33) | 8<br>(26.67) | 1<br>(3.33) | 0<br>(0.00) | 30<br>(100.00) |
| Bulk Supply | 4<br>(66.67) | 4<br>(66.67) | 2<br>(33.33) | 3<br>(50.00) | 0<br>(0.00) | 0<br>(0.00) | 6<br>(100.00) |
| Street Lighting | 2<br>(66.67) | 2<br>(66.67) | 0<br>(0.00) | 2<br>(66.67) | 1<br>(33.33) | 0<br>(0.00) | 3<br>(100.00) |
| Total | 196<br>(78.71) | 143<br>(57.43) | 120<br>(48.19) | 70<br>(28.11) | 36<br>(14.46) | 6<br>(2.41) | 249<br>(100.00) |

*Note*: Figures in parentheses show percentages.
*Source*: Field Survey.

It is generally found that farmers use their tube well connections for domestic purposes at their farmhouses. In our survey we found that 90 per cent of the consumers agreed that the tube well connection was used for domestic purposes. Another 20 per cent of them mentioned that it was used for the lighting of bulbs and tubes. About 17 per cent mentioned that fans, coolers, etc., were also run on the same connections. More than one-half of the consumers (53 per cent) were of the view that the farmers used all domestic equipment like bulbs, fans, coolers, refrigerators, heaters, etc. Only 3 consumers (10 per cent) mentioned that farmers were not using any of this equipment at their farmhouses.

The following inferences emerge from the above analysis of the perceptions of the consumers:

1. The consumers clearly identified that low voltage and frequent trippings were due to the overloading of transformers and the poor quality of maintenance of the transmission and distribution systems.
2. Consumers indulge in power theft to avoid having to pay for electricity consumption. They do so because, despite having the capacity to pay, they know that there is no effective check and that they can get away with it.
3. Consumers believed that more than any other category of consumers, the industrialists indulge in the theft of power to escape payment of dues. They did not concede that power theft occurred in the agricultural sector, although they strongly preferred metered supply to the flat rate system. However, agricultural consumers were strongly in favour of the flat rate system.
4. People of all socio-economic backgrounds indulge in the theft of power. However, it was more so in the case of people who enjoyed political backing and the patronage of higher officers.
5. A large majority of consumers believed that pilferage was not possible without the active connivance or knowledge of the employees. Involvement of employees was quite widespread, through lower-ranking employees like linemen; meter readers were more involved than the higher officers. The employees who connive in the pilferage of power generally enjoy the backing of local politicians and higher officers and enter into mutually beneficial contracts with consumers, both in cash and in kind.
6. Tampering with meters, the use of *kundies* direct supply, and

the use of defective meters were the three major ways to pilfer power. To check this, tamper-proof sealing of meters, quick replacement of defective/burntout meters, monetary fines, disconnections, frequent checking, fixing individual responsibility, breaking the nexus between corrupt employees and unscrupulous consumers by the regular transfers of the field staff, and providing incentives for detecting power theft were identified as effective methods to control the pilferage of power.

7. The majority of the consumers identified the high tariff rates as an important factor inducing people to indulge in power theft. However, quite a significant number of respondents (26 per cent) believed that tariff rates were not as important a factor as the quality of supply and availability on demand.
8. Most of the farmers install bigger motors than the sanctioned load. They use various machines, both legally allowed or otherwise. They use these for domestic consumption at farmhouses, etc.
9. A majority of consumers of all categories was in favour of the privatization of the distribution of power. In particular, an overwhelming majority of industrial consumers was strongly in favour of privatization. The reasons put forward were that it would involve less corruption and would improve the quality of service. However, the majority was in favour of a subsidized supply of power to the agricultural sector.
10. Consumers were quite sceptical about the involvement of community-based organizations such as gram panchayats and municipal committees. They believed that they would be sectarian in their approach as they were highly politicized and would not be judicious in their decisions. Respondents were also not enthusiastic about involving other organizations like youth clubs, mahila mandals, Rotary Clubs, etc.
11. Almost all the respondents believed that the theft of power was a bad practice and should be discouraged. Consumers favoured various communication methods to highlight the evil effects of the pilferage of power. They strongly favoured public meetings and a process of collective decision-making which would provide a sense of participation and engender a sense of moral obligation/commitment among the participants. This would lead to their public exposure and discourage them from pilfering in the

future. Publicity through radio and television was suggested as the other important channel for increasing public awareness and raising public consciousness.

12. For increased consumer satisfaction, they pleaded for adequate and uninterrupted supply of power, quick redressal of grievances, reduction in tariff, and frequent meetings with officers.

CHAPTER 5

# Perceptions of Punjab Employees Regarding Theft of Power

In the previous chapter, we studied the perceptions of the consumers in relation to the problems of the theft of power and the conservation of energy, the various methods employed by unscrupulous consumers to steal power and the ways to check this menace, the effectiveness of the existing organizational structure, the tariff structure, issues of accountability and responsiveness, and community-based intervention strategies.

In this chapter, we shall study the perceptions of the employees regarding the issues related to the pilferage of power and the conservation of energy on lines similar to the analysis of the consumers' perceptions. The chapter is divided into six sections.

Section 1 deals with the perceptions of the employees regarding the attitude of the people/consumers towards the problem of power theft and conservation of power.

Section 2 deals with various methods used by consumers to pilfer power and methods to check such pilferage, as well as suggestions regarding new methods to plug the existing loopholes.

Section 3 deals with the views of the employees regarding the impact of the existing tariff rates on the pilferage of power.

Section 4 deals with perceptions of employees regarding the efficacy of the existing systems of supervision, enforcement, and accountability. It includes a discussion on the existing supervision and inspection system, the penal system, the nature of problems encountered in enforcing the existing rules to check pilferage of power, and the nature of consumer resistance, etc.

Section 5 describes the perceptions of employees regarding community-based intervention strategies.

Section 6 deals with perceptions regarding the nature and role of incentives for the employees, the role of employees' unions, additional powers and motivational steps for the employees, and the nature and type of technical and moral training programmes for the employees.

First, we shall discuss briefly the main problems faced by the employees at their workplace as well as the problems they encounter in relation to the distribution of electricity to the consumers and the reasons for the same as perceived by the employees.

Table 5.1 presents the key problems faced by the employees at their workplace. The main problem was found to be the shortage of maintenance materials as expressed by a large majority of the employees (72 per cent), which included all SEs, 67 per cent of the XENs, 92 per cent of the SDOs, 72 per cent of the JEs, 77 per cent of the linemen, and 57 per cent of the meter readers. Closely related to the problem of the shortage of maintenance materials was the problem of sub-standard materials, as mentioned by 36 per cent of the employees. Shortage of staff was another problem mentioned by about one-half of the employees. Other relatively less important problems mentioned by the employees were: lack of tools (T&P) (34 per cent), lack of incentives/overtime/promotions (15 per cent), lack of cooperation from higher officials (11 per cent), and the problem of transport (10 per cent).

The employees were asked to identify the main problems in the distribution of electricity to consumers (Table 5.2). Low voltage was identified as the main problem confronting the consumers, as revealed by a large majority of them (68 per cent). Low voltage often resulted in breakdowns/trippings or resulted in the irregular supply to the consumers. Old distribution lines was another problem and it was mentioned by one-third of the employees. Still another problem was planned and unplanned cuts, mentioned by 17 per cent of the employees. However, 11 per cent of the employees were of the view that the consumers did not face any problem.

Problems such as low voltage, old distribution lines, frequent breakdowns or trippings, etc., result in poor service to the consumers. We asked the employees what they perceived were the reasons for the poor service. Their perceptions are shown in Table 5.3. The most important reason as identified by a majority of employees (74 per cent) was the overloading of transformers. The overloading of transformers caused low voltage, which in turn resulted in frequent breakdowns or trippings. Shortage of maintenance staff and poor maintenance of the distribution network were mentioned by 31 per cent and 30 per cent of the employees respectively. Other reasons

TABLE 5.1: KEY PROBLEMS FACED BY EMPLOYEES AT THEIR WORKPLACE

| Category of Employee | Lack of T & P | Shortage of Maintenance Material | Sub-Standard Material | Lack of Co-operation | Lack of Incentives Overtime, Promotions | Problem of Transport | Shortge of Staff | Total Res-pondents |
|---|---|---|---|---|---|---|---|---|
| SE | 0 | 3 | 0 | 1 | 0 | 0 | 2 | 3 |
| | 0.00 | (100.00) | (0.00) | (33.33) | (0.00) | (0.00) | (66.67) | (100.00) |
| XEN | 3 | 4 | 2 | 0 | 0 | 0 | 2 | 6 |
| | (50.00) | (66.67) | (33.33) | (0.00) | (0.00) | (0.00) | (33.33) | (100.00) |
| SDO | 3 | 11 | 6 | 2 | 1 | 1 | 7 | 12 |
| | (25.00) | (91.67) | (50.00) | (16.67) | (8.33) | (8.33) | (58.33) | (100.00) |
| JE | 7 | 13 | 8 | 1 | 1 | 4 | 9 | 18 |
| | (38.89) | (72.22) | (44.44) | (5.56) | (5.56) | (22.22) | (50.00) | (100.00) |
| Linemen | 16 | 23 | 11 | 2 | 1 | 2 | 15 | 30 |
| | (53.33) | (76.67) | (36.67) | (6.67) | (3:33) | (6.67) | (50.00) | (100.00) |
| Meter Reader | 5 | 17 | 9 | 5 | 12 | 3 | 14 | 30 |
| | (16.67) | (56.67) | (30.00) | (16.67) | (40.00) | (10.00) | (46.67) | (100.00) |
| All | 34 | 71 | 36 | 11 | 15 | 10 | 49 | 99 |
| | (34.34) | (71.72) | (36.36) | (11.11) | (15.15) | (10.10) | (49.49) | (100.00) |

*Note*: Figures in parentheses show percentages.
*Source*: Field Survey.

TABLE 5.2: MAIN PROBLEM IN THE DISTRIBUTION OF ELECTRICITY TO CONSUMERS

| Category of Employee | Old Distribution Lines | Low Voltage | Planned & Unplanned Power | No Problem | Total Respon-dents |
|---|---|---|---|---|---|
| SE | 0 | 3 | 1 | 0 | 3 |
| | 0.00 | (100.00) | (33.33) | 0.00 | (100.00) |
| XEN | 1 | 3 | 0 | 3 | 6 |
| | (16.67) | (50.00) | 0.00 | (50.00) | (100.00) |
| SDO | 6 | 5 | 1 | 2 | 12 |
| | (50.00) | (41.67) | (8.33) | (16.67) | (100.00) |
| JE | 8 | 14 | 4 | 2 | 18 |
| | (44.44) | (77.78) | (22.22) | (11.11) | (100.00) |
| Lineman | 7 | 14 | 6 | 4 | 30 |
| | (23.33) | (46.67) | (20.00) | (13.33) | (100.00) |
| Meter Reader | 11 | 28 | 5 | 0 | 30 |
| | (36.67) | (93.33) | (16.67) | (0.00) | (100.00) |
| All | 33 | 67 | 17 | 11 | 99 |
| | (33.33) | (67.68) | (17.17) | (11.11) | (100.00) |

*Note*: Figures in parentheses show percentages.
*Source*: Field Survey.

mentioned were inadequate supply (13 per cent) and negligence on the part of the employees (6 per cent).

## 1. ATTITUDE TOWARDS POWER THEFT

The perceptions of employees regarding why people indulge in theft of power are presented in Table 5.4. A majority of the employees (58 per cent) mentioned the desire of people to save money by avoiding or reducing their obligation to pay for consumption as the main reason. These employees included 67 per cent of the SEs, 50 per cent of the XENs, 83 per cent of the SDOs, 56 per cent of the JEs, 53 per cent of the linemen, and 57 per cent of the meter readers. The other important reason, mentioned by about 40 per cent of the employees, was the high rate of tariff. Other relatively less important reasons mentioned were inadequate supply of power (21 per cent), habitual practice (21 per cent), and any other (7 per cent) such as incorrect bills, etc., and 3 per cent of the employees did not know why people indulged in theft of power. The employees were also asked whether there was a relation between theft of power and difficulty in getting a

TABLE 5.3: REASONS FOR THE POOR QUALITY OF SERVICE OF ELECTRICITY TO CONSUMERS

| Category of Employee | Inadequate Supply | Overloading of Transformers | Poor Maintenance of Distribution Network | Shortage of Maintenance Staff | Negligence of Employees | No Problem | Total Respondents |
|---|---|---|---|---|---|---|---|
| SE | 0 | 2 | 0 | 0 | 0 | 0 | 3 |
| | 0.00 | (66.67) | (0.00) | (0.00) | (0.00) | (0.00) | (100.00) |
| XEN | 0 | 4 | 0 | 1 | 1 | 2 | 6 |
| | 0.00 | (66.67) | (0.00) | (16.67) | (16.67) | (33.33) | (100.00) |
| SDO | 0 | 10 | 6 | 4 | 2 | 2 | 12 |
| | 0.00 | (83.33) | (50.00) | (33.33) | (16.67) | (16.67) | (100.00) |
| JE | 6 | 13 | 7 | 5 | 2 | 2 | 18 |
| | (33.33) | (72.22) | (38.89) | (27.78) | (11.11) | (11.11) | (100.00) |
| Lineman | 3 | 20 | 8 | 8 | 0 | 3 | 30 |
| | (10.00) | (66.67) | (26.67) | (26.67) | (0.00) | (10.00) | (100.00) |
| Meter Reader | 4 | 24 | 9 | 13 | 1 | 1 | 30 |
| | (13.33) | (80.00) | (30.00) | (43.33) | (3.33) | (3.33) | (100.00) |
| All | 13 | 73 | 30 | 31 | 6 | 10 | 99 |
| | (13.13) | (73.74) | (30.30) | (31.31) | (6.06) | (10.10) | (100.00) |

*Note*: Figures in parentheses show percentages.
*Source*: Field Survey.

TABLE 5.4: REASONS FOR THEFT OF POWER BY CONSUMERS

| Category of Employee | Inadequate Supply | Saving of Money | High Tariff Rates | Habitual Practice | Any Other | Don't Know | Total Respondents |
|---|---|---|---|---|---|---|---|
| SE | 1 | 2 | 1 | 0 | 0 | 0 | 3 |
| | (33.33) | (66.67) | (33.33) | (0.00) | (0.00) | (0.00) | (100.00) |
| XEN | 0 | 3 | 0 | 3 | 1 | 1 | 6 |
| | 0.00 | (50.00) | (0.00) | (50.00) | (16.67) | (16.67) | (100.00) |
| SDO | 0 | 10 | 3 | 7 | 1 | 0 | 12 |
| | 0.00 | (83.33) | (25.00) | (58.33) | (8.33) | (0.00) | (100.00) |
| JE | 3 | 10 | 8 | 3 | 1 | 2 | 18 |
| | (16.67) | (55.56) | (44.44) | (16.67) | (5.56) | (11.11) | (100.00) |
| Lineman | 7 | 16 | 13 | 3 | 4 | 0 | 30 |
| | (23.33) | (53.33) | (43.33) | (10.00) | (13.33) | (0.00) | (100.00) |
| Meter Reader | 10 | 17 | 14 | 5 | 0 | 0 | 30 |
| | (33.33) | (56.67) | (46.67) | (16.67) | (0.00) | (0.00) | (100.00) |
| All | 21 | 58 | 39 | 21 | 7 | 3 | 99 |
| | (21.21) | (58.59) | (39.39) | (21.21) | (7.07) | (3.03) | (100.00) |

*Note*: Figures in parentheses show percentages.
*Source*: Field Survey.

legal connection. A large majority of them mentioned that there was a positive relation between the two.

The employees were asked at what time of the day power theft was most frequently committed. A great majority of the employees (83 per cent) felt that theft was committed at night when there was little checking, and 15 per cent of them mentioned that it was committed at any time of the day. (And only 1 per cent mentioned that it was committed during the day.) As to the season in which theft was most frequently committed, a majority of the employees (55 per cent) mentioned that it was committed throughout the year, 41 per cent mentioned summer time, and 2 per cent mentioned winter time.

The employees were asked which category of consumers indulged relatively more frequently in the pilferage of power (Table 5.5). About 40 per cent of them were of the view that industrial consumers committed more theft. Employees holding this view included 33 per cent of the SEs, 17 per cent of the SDOs, 24 per cent of the JEs, 63 per cent of the linemen, and 37 per cent of the meter readers. Another 38 per cent mentioned that domestic consumers committed more theft and claimed that this section included police colonies. In fact, during

TABLE 5.5: CATEGORY OF CONSUMERS INDULGING IN THEFT OF POWER

| Category | Domestic | Commercial | Agri-cultural | Industrial | Total Respon-dents |
|---|---|---|---|---|---|
| SE | 2 | 0 | 0 | 1 | 3 |
| | (66.67) | (0.00) | (0.00) | (33.33) | (100.00) |
| XEN | 3 | 1 | 2 | 0 | 6 |
| | (50.00) | (16.67) | (33.33) | (0.00) | (100.00) |
| SDO | 7 | 1 | 2 | 2 | 12 |
| | (58.33) | (8.33) | (16.67) | (16.67) | (100.00) |
| JE | 9 | 0 | 2 | 7 | 18 |
| | (50.00) | (0.00) | (11.11) | (38.89) | (100.00) |
| Lineman | 8 | 0 | 3 | 19 | 30 |
| | (26.67) | (0.00) | (10.00) | (63.33) | (100.00) |
| Meter Reader | 9 | 1 | 9 | 11 | 30 |
| | (30.00) | (3.33) | (30.00) | (36.67) | (100.00) |
| All | 38 | 3 | 18 | 40 | 99 |
| | (38.38) | (3.03) | (18.18) | (40.40) | (100.00) |

*Note*: Figures in parentheses show percentages.
*Source*: Field Survey.

our survey the employees revealed that the police department indulged more in the pilferage of power than the other groups of consumers. Agricultural consumers committed more theft according to 18 per cent of the employees. Only 3 per cent of the employees were of the view that commercial consumers committed more theft.

As regards the social background of the people committing such theft, a majority of the employees (78 per cent) mentioned that people of all castes were involved. Another significant section of the employees (19 per cent) was of the opinion that only the upper caste people were involved. As regards the educational background of the people indulging in the theft of power, about 47 per cent of the employees were of the view that both educated and uneducated people were involved. According to 35 per cent of the employees, such people had an education ranging between the middle standard and below the graduation level. According to 10 per cent of the employees, people with education up to the graduation level or more were involved. Only 4 per cent of the employees mentioned that illiterate persons also committed theft of power. On the issue of the economic background of people committing theft of power, the employees were found to be divided. According to 44 per cent of the employees, people from all strata (rich and poor) committed theft of electricity. Another 37 per cent of them mentioned that only the rich were involved, and 17 per cent of them were of the view that only the middle class people were involved. In regard to the political background of the people indulging in theft of power, a large majority of the employees (72 per cent) mentioned that only politically influential people committed theft of power. These employees included all the SEs, 33 per cent of the XENs, 67 per cent of the SDOs, 71 per cent of the JEs, and 70 per cent each of the linemen and meter readers. According to 22 per cent of them, these people did not have any politically influential background, and 5 per cent of them expressed ignorance about the matter. This clearly shows that persons with political links or background indulge in theft of power more than the others.

To assess the level of awareness regarding wastage of power and energy conservation measures, the respondent employees were asked questions on the ways in which the consumers wasted power. Table 5.6 gives the perceptions of the employees in this regard. An overwhelming majority (94 per cent) of the employees were of the view that the consumers wasted power through unnecessary use of it such as keeping the lights, fans, etc., on even when not required.

TABLE 5.6: WAYS IN WHICH CONSUMERS WASTE POWER (KNOWLEDGE OF ENERGY CONSERVATION MEASURES)

| Category of Employee | Ostentatious use during Ceremonies | Un-necessary use | Use of Appliances of Higher Wattage than is Required | Lack of Knowledge of Energy Efficient Appliances | Total Respon-dents |
|---|---|---|---|---|---|
| SE | 0 | 3 | 1 | 0 | 3 |
| | (0.00) | (100.00) | (33.33) | 0.00 | (100.00) |
| XEN | 0 | 6 | 4 | 2 | 6 |
| | (0.00) | (100.00) | (66.67) | (33.33) | (100.00) |
| SDO | 3 | 12 | 6 | 5 | 12 |
| | (25.00) | (100.00) | (50.00) | (41.67) | (100.00) |
| JE | 2 | 19 | 8 | 3 | 18 |
| | (11.11) | (105.56) | (44.44) | (16.67) | (100.00) |
| Lineman | 4 | 28 | 10 | 6 | 30 |
| | (13.33) | (93.33) | (33.33) | (20.00) | (100.00) |
| Meter Reader | 2 | 25 | 13 | 4 | 30 |
| | (6.67) | (83.33) | (43.33) | (13.33) | (100.00) |
| All | 11 | 93 | 42 | 20 | 99 |
| | (11.11) | (93.94) | (42.42) | (20.20) | (100.00) |

*Note*: Figures in parentheses show percentages.
*Source*: Field Survey.

About 42 per cent of the employees mentioned the use of appliances of higher wattage than was required as the other important reason. Some employees mentioned lack of knowledge about energy-efficient appliances (20 per cent) and showing off on public ceremonies and functions (11 per cent) as the other ways in which consumers wasted power.

Table 5.7 shows the perceptions of the employees regarding the involvement of employees in the theft of power. It is generally believed that power theft is not possible without the connivance of the employees. In our survey, about 82 per cent of the employees agreed that employees were involved in one way or the other in the theft of power. Employees who hold this view include all SEs, 83 per cent of the XENs, 83 per cent of the SDOs, 67 per cent of the JEs, 73 per cent of the linemen, and 83 per cent of the meter readers. However, 16 per cent of the employees felt that employees were not involved in the theft of power. Only 2 per cent of the employees expressed ignorance regarding such involvement.

TABLE 5.7: INVOLVEMENT OF EMPLOYEES IN THEFT OF POWER

| Category of Employee | Involved | Not Involved | Dont't Know | Total Respondents |
|---|---|---|---|---|
| SE | 3<br>(100.00) | 0<br>(0.00) | 0<br>(0.00) | 3<br>(100.00) |
| XEN | 5<br>(83.33) | 1<br>(16.67) | 0<br>(0.00) | 6<br>(100.00) |
| SDO | 10<br>(83.33) | 1<br>(8.33) | 1<br>(8.33) | 12<br>(100.00) |
| JE | 16<br>(88.89) | 2<br>(11.11) | 0<br>(0.00) | 18<br>(100.00) |
| Lineman | 22<br>(73.33) | 7<br>(23.33) | 1<br>(3.33) | 30<br>(100.00) |
| Meter Reader | 25<br>(83.33) | 5<br>(16.67) | 0<br>(0.00) | 30<br>(100.00) |
| All | 81<br>(81.82) | 16<br>(16.16) | 2<br>(2.02) | 99<br>(100.00) |

*Note*: Figures in parentheses show percentages.
*Source*: Field Survey.

Table 5.8 shows the extent of involvement of the employees (i.e. the percentage of employees involved). A majority of the employees (51 per cent) were of the view that the employees were involved to a small extent, while 33 per cent of them felt that the employees were involved to a large extent, and 14 per cent of them claimed that the employees were not involved at all.

The employees were divided on the issue of the official level or rank of the employees involved in the theft of power (Table 5.9). According to 30 per cent of them, only the lower-level employees (below JEs) were involved in the theft of power. In contrast to the lower-level employees, more high-level employees perceived that lower-level employees were involved in the theft of power. However, 28 per cent of the employees were of the view that only higher-level employees (JEs and above) were involved.

Regarding the nature of contracts (bribes, etc.) entered into by the employees involved in the theft of power with the consumers (Table 5.10), a majority of the employees (59 per cent) mentioned that it involved transactions both in cash and kind. According 21 per cent of them, it involved only cash, while 4 per cent mentioned that it involved only transactions in kind.

TABLE 5.8: EXTENT OF INVOLVEMENT OF EMPLOYEES IN THEFT OF POWER

| Category of Employee | Large | Small | No Involvement | Total Respondents |
|---|---|---|---|---|
| SE | 1 | 2 | 0 | 3 |
| | (33.33) | (66.67) | 0.00 | (100.00) |
| XEN | 0 | 5 | 1 | 6 |
| | 0.00 | (83.33) | (16.67) | (100.00) |
| SDO | 5 | 6 | 1 | 12 |
| | (41.67) | (50.00) | (8.33) | (100.00) |
| JE | 8 | 8 | 2 | 18 |
| | (44.44) | (44.44) | (11.11) | (100.00) |
| Lineman | 9 | 15 | 6 | 30 |
| | (30.00) | (50.00) | (20.00) | (100.00) |
| Meter Reader | 10 | 15 | 5 | 30 |
| | (33.33) | (50.00) | (16.67) | (100.00) |
| All | 33 | 51 | 15 | 99 |
| | (33.33) | (51.52) | (15.15) | (100.00) |

*Note*: Figures in parentheses show percentages.
*Source*: Field Survey.

Generally, the employees who are involved in the theft of power enjoy some protection or backing. Table 5.11 describes the perceptions of the employees regarding the backing enjoyed by the employees involved in the theft of power. As is clear from the table, 43 per cent of them were of the opinion that such employees enjoyed the patronage of both higher-level officials and local politicians. Another 16 per cent of them mentioned that they enjoyed the protection of only higher officials, while 10 per cent of them mentioned that they enjoyed the backing only of local politicians. About 30 per cent of them felt that such employees did not enjoy any backing and operated on their own.

## 2. METHODS USED TO PILFER POWER AND METHODS USED TO CHECK IT

As regards the methods of committing theft of power by consumers, the main methods (Table 5.12) include tampering of meters and these of defective meters, according to the majority of the employees (51 per cent). Use of *kundis* or direct supply from the lines was another method mentioned by about 35 per cent of the employees. Another 40 per cent of the employees mentioned that all these

TABLE 5.9: OFFICIAL LEVEL OF EMPLOYEES INVOLVED IN THEFT OF POWER

| Category of Consumer | Highter Level (Above JE) | Lower Level (Below JE) | All Involved | No Involvement | Don't Know/ | Total Respondents |
|---|---|---|---|---|---|---|
| SE | 1 | 2 | 0 | 0 | 0 | 3 |
| | (33.33) | (66.67) | (0.00) | (0.00) | (0.00) | (100.00) |
| XEN | 0 | 4 | 1 | 1 | 0 | 6 |
| | (0.00) | (66.67) | (16.67) | (16.67) | (0.00) | (100.00) |
| SDO | 2 | 5 | 3 | 1 | 1 | 12 |
| | (16.67) | (41.67) | (25.00) | (8.33) | (8.33) | (100.00) |
| JE | 2 | 9 | 6 | 1 | 0 | 18 |
| | (11.11) | (50.00) | (33.33) | (5.56) | (0.00) | (100.00) |
| Lineman | 12 | 5 | 7 | 4 | 2 | 30 |
| | (40.00) | (16.67) | (23.33) | (13.33) | (6.67) | (100.00) |
| Meter Reader | 11 | 5 | 9 | 4 | 1 | 30 |
| | (36.67) | (16.67) | (30.00) | (13.33) | (3.33) | (100.00) |
| All | 28 | 30 | 26 | 11 | 4 | 99 |
| | (28.28) | (30.30) | (26.26) | (11.11) | (4.04) | (100.00) |

*Note*: Figures in parentheses show percentages.
*Source*: Field Survey.

TABLE 5.10: NATURE OF BENEFICIAL CONTRACTS (BRIBES, ETC.) BETWEEN EMPLOYEES AND CONSUMERS

| Category of Employee | Cash | Kind | Both Cash & Kind | No Involvement | Total Respondents |
|---|---|---|---|---|---|
| SE | 1<br>(33.33) | 0<br>(0.00) | 1<br>(33.33) | 1<br>(33.33) | 3<br>(100.00) |
| XEN | 0<br>(0.00) | 0<br>(0.00) | 5<br>(83.33) | 0<br>(0.00) | 6<br>(100.00) |
| SDO | 1<br>(8.33) | 0<br>(0.00) | 8<br>(66.67) | 3<br>(25.00) | 12<br>(100.00) |
| JE | 2<br>(11.11) | 1<br>(5.56) | 14<br>(77.78) | 1<br>(5.56) | 18<br>(100.00) |
| Lineman | 11<br>(36.67) | 1<br>(3.33) | 13<br>(43.33) | 5<br>(16.67) | 30<br>(100.00) |
| Meter Reader | 6<br>(20.00) | 2<br>(6.67) | 17<br>(56.67) | 5<br>(16.67) | 30<br>(100.00) |
| ALL | 21<br>(21.21) | 4<br>(4.04) | 58<br>(58.59) | 15<br>(15.15) | 99<br>(100.00) |

*Note*: Figures in parentheses show percentages.
*Source*: Field Survey.

TABLE 5.11: BACKING/PROTECTION ENJOYED BY EMPLOYEES INVOLVED IN THEFT OF POWER

| Category of Employee | Local Politicians | Higher Officials | Both Local Politicians and Higher Officials | No Backing | Total Respondents |
|---|---|---|---|---|---|
| SE | 0<br>(0.00) | 0<br>(0.00) | 1<br>(33.33) | 2<br>(66.67) | 3<br>(100.00) |
| XEN | 1<br>(16.67) | 2<br>(33.33) | 2<br>(33.33) | 1<br>(16.67) | 6<br>(100.00) |
| SDO | 3<br>(25.00) | 3<br>(25.00) | 3<br>(25.00) | 3<br>(25.00) | 12<br>(100.00) |
| JE | 2<br>(11.11) | 2<br>(11.11) | 7<br>(38.89) | 7<br>(38.89) | 18<br>(100.00) |
| Lineman | 3<br>(10.00) | 6<br>(20.00) | 13<br>(43.33) | 8<br>(26.67) | 30<br>(100.00) |
| Meter Reader | 1<br>(3.33) | 3<br>(10.00) | 17<br>(56.67) | 9<br>(30.00) | 30<br>(100.00) |
| ALL | 10<br>(10.10) | 16<br>(16.16) | 43<br>(43.43) | 30<br>(30.30) | 99<br>(100.00) |

*Note*: Figures in parentheses show percentages.
*Source*: Field Survey.

TABLE 5.12: METHODS OF COMMITTING THEFT OF POWER

| Category of Employee | Tampering of Meters | Defective Meters | Use of *Kundies*/Direct Supply | All of These | Any Others | Total Respondents |
|---|---|---|---|---|---|---|
| SE | 1<br>(33.33) | 0<br>(0.00) | 0<br>(0.00) | 2<br>(66.67) | 0<br>(0.00) | 3<br>(100.00) |
| XEN | 3<br>(50.00) | 1<br>(16.67) | 1<br>(16.67) | 3<br>(50.00) | 0<br>(0.00) | 6<br>(100.00) |
| SDO | 5<br>(41.67) | 3<br>(25.00) | 2<br>(16.67) | 6<br>(50.00) | 0<br>(0.00) | 12<br>(100.00) |
| JE | 10<br>(55.56) | 0<br>(0.00) | 7<br>(38.89) | 7<br>(38.89) | 1<br>(5.56) | 18<br>(100.00) |
| Lineman | 13<br>(43.33) | 5<br>(16.67) | 11<br>(36.67) | 13<br>(43.33) | 3<br>(10.00) | 30<br>(100.00) |
| Meter Reader | 18<br>(60.00) | 2<br>(6.67) | 14<br>(46.67) | 9<br>(30.00) | 2<br>(6.67) | 30<br>(100.00) |
| ALL | 50<br>(50.51) | 11<br>(11.11) | 35<br>(35.35) | 40<br>(40.40) | 6<br>(6.06) | 99<br>(100.00) |

*Note*: Figures in parentheses show percentages.
*Source*: Field Survey.

methods were used. Only 6 per cent of them mentioned methods other than these.

There are several methods to check theft of power, which can be categorized as:

1. Technical methods
2. Organizational methods
3. Social methods
4. Changes in the tariff structure
5. Checking by the staff

1. *Technical methods:* These methods relate to improvements, in the sealing system of meters, replacement of burnt out or defective meters quickly, etc. In our survey (Table 5.13), a majority of the employees (62 per cent) suggested improvements in the sealing system of meters and joints as the most effective method of checking theft of power. Improvement in the sealing system involves not just the proper sealing of meters but also of naked joints in the distribution lines.

TABLE 5.13: TECHNICAL METHODS OF CONTAINING THEFT OF POWER

| Category of Employee | Improve Sealing System of Meters/ Joints | Replace Burnt/ Defective Meters Immediately | Install Meters at one point in Village/ Locality | Any Other | Total Respondents |
|---|---|---|---|---|---|
| SE | 1 | 0 | 1 | 0 | 3 |
| | (33.33) | 0.00 | (33.33) | (0.00) | (100.00) |
| XEN | 3 | 1 | 1 | 0 | 6 |
| | (50.00) | (16.67) | (16.67) | (0.00) | (100.00) |
| SDO | 7 | 1 | 8 | 2 | 12 |
| | (58.33) | (8.33) | (66.67) | (16.67) | (100.00) |
| JE | 10 | 4 | 10 | 0 | 18 |
| | (55.56) | (22.22) | (55.56) | (0.00) | (100.00) |
| Lineman | 20 | 6 | 14 | 5 | 30 |
| | (66.67) | (20.00) | (46.67) | (16.67) | (100.00) |
| Meter Reader | 21 | 5 | 17 | 3 | 30 |
| | (70.00) | (16.67) | (56.67) | (10.00) | (100.00) |
| ALL | 62 | 17 | 51 | 10 | 99 |
| | (62.63) | (17.17) | (51.52) | (10.10) | (100.00) |

*Note*: Figures in parentheses show percentages.
*Source*: Field Survey.

Another method suggested by 51 per cent of the employees was the installation of meters at one point in the village or locality outside the reach of the consumers. Still another method related to the immediate replacement of burnt out or defective meters and this was suggested by 17 per cent of the employees. About 10 per cent of the employees suggested other methods such as providing electricity to the consumers at a flat rate, etc.

2. *Organizational methods*: These methods involve fixing the responsibility of the employees, the regular transfer of the employees to avoid establishing a nexus between them and the consumers, granting incentives to the employees, the enforcement of strict punishment, the involvement of the employees' union, etc. In the course of our survey (Table 5.14) we found that 47 per cent of the employees favoured more incentives to the employees as an important step towards checking power theft. About 40 per cent of them suggested that the responsibility of each employee should be fixed. Another 38 per cent suggested the regular transfer of the checking staff to avoid a nexus between the consumers and the employees. Another 22 per cent of them suggested that strict punishment should be awarded to the culprits. Only 7 per cent of the employees suggested other methods such as the flat rate system, privatization of the PSEB, etc., as means of checking the theft of power.

3. *Social methods*: Social methods of checking the theft of power involve creating social awareness among the people regarding the ill effects of power theft, exposing in public those who indulge in the theft, etc. Our findings (Table 5.15) show that a majority of the employees (65 per cent) stressed the need for both creating social awareness among the people and exposing the guilty in public as effective methods of checking theft. They included 70 per cent of the meter readers, 53 per cent of the linemen, 78 per cent of the JEs, 67 per cent each of the SDOs and XENs, and 33 per cent of the SEs. Another 16 per cent of the employees suggested only the creation of social awareness among the people, and 17 per cent suggested only exposing the guilty in public.

4. *Changes in the tariff structure*: The high rate of tariff was indicated to be one of the important causes of the theft of power.

TABLE 5.14: ORGANIZATIONAL METHODS OF CONTAINING THEFT OF POWER

| Category of Employee | Responsibility of each Employee be Fixed | Regular Transfer of Employees | Incentives | Strict Punishment | Any Other | Total Respondents |
|---|---|---|---|---|---|---|
| SE | 1 | 1 | 0 | 2 | 0 | 3 |
| | (33.33) | (33.33) | (0.00) | (66.67) | (0.00) | (100.00) |
| XEN | 2 | 3 | 3 | 3 | 0 | 6 |
| | (33.33) | (50.00) | (50.00) | (50.00) | (0.00) | (100.00) |
| SDO | 5 | 7 | 5 | 1 | 1 | 12 |
| | (41.67) | (58.33) | (41.67) | (8.33) | (8.33) | (100.00) |
| JE | 4 | 5 | 9 | 3 | 3 | 18 |
| | (22.22) | (27.78) | (50.00) | (16.67) | (16.67) | (100.00) |
| Lineman | 12 | 9 | 16 | 6 | 3 | 30 |
| | (40.00) | (30.00) | (53.33) | (20.00) | (10.00) | (100.00) |
| Meter Reader | 16 | 13 | 14 | 7 | 2 | 30 |
| | (53.33) | (43.33) | (46.67) | (23.33) | (6.67) | (100.00) |
| All | 40 | 38 | 47 | 22 | 9 | 99 |
| | (40.40) | (38.38) | (47.47) | (22.22) | (9.09) | (100.00) |

*Note*: Figures in parentheses show percentages.
*Source*: Field Survey.

TABLE 5.15: SOCIAL METHDOS OF CONTAINING THEFT OF POWER

| Category of Employee | Social Awareness among People | Expose People in Public | Both Social Awareness & Public Exposure | Don't Know | Total Respon-dents |
|---|---|---|---|---|---|
| SE | 0<br>(0.00) | 0<br>(0.00) | 1<br>(33.33) | 0<br>(0.00) | 3<br>(100.00) |
| XEN | 1<br>(16.67) | 2<br>(33.33) | 4<br>(66.67) | 0<br>(0.00) | 6<br>(100.00) |
| SDO | 2<br>(16.67) | 1<br>(8.33) | 8<br>(66.67) | 0<br>(0.00) | 12<br>(100.00) |
| JE | 2<br>(11.11) | 2<br>(11.11) | 14<br>(77.78) | 1<br>(5.56) | 18<br>(100.00) |
| Lineman | 7<br>(23.33) | 7<br>(23.33) | 16<br>(53.33) | 2<br>(6.67) | 30<br>(100.00) |
| Meter Reader | 4<br>(13.33) | 5<br>(16.67) | 21<br>(70.00) | 2<br>(6.67) | 30<br>(100.00) |
| ALL | 16<br>(16.16) | 17<br>(17.17) | 64<br>(64.65) | 5<br>(5.05) | 99<br>(100.00) |

*Note*: Figures in parentheses show percentages.
*Source*: Field Survey.

Accordingly, a majority of the employees (53 per cent) suggested a reduction in the tariff rates as an effective method of checking power theft (Table 5.16). Another 23 per cent of the employees held the view that the tariff should not be changed but instead the quality of the supply should be improved. According to 9 per cent of the employees, changes in the tariff structure would be of little use in checking theft of power. Another 21 per cent of the employees were in favour of increasing the monthly minimum charges to discourage people from indulging in the theft of power.

5. *Checking by the staff*: Checking by the staff was another method suggested by the employees to reduce pilferage of power (Table 5.17). A majority of the employees suggested frequent checking and random checking by the staff (51 per cent each). Another 36 per cent of them suggested that there should be both frequent and random checking.

TABLE 5.16: CHANGES IN TARIFF STRUCTURE TO CHECK THEFT OF POWER

| Category of of Employee | Monthly Minimum Charges be Increased | Tariff should be Reduced | No Effect of Tariff Change | No Change in Tariff but Quality of Supply be Increased | Total Respondents |
|---|---|---|---|---|---|
| SE | 0 | 1 | 2 | 0 | 3 |
| | (0.00) | (33.33) | (66.67) | (0.00) | (100.00) |
| XEN | 0 | 3 | 0 | 3 | 6 |
| | (0.00) | (50.00) | (0.00) | (50.00) | (100.00) |
| SDO | 3 | 6 | 1 | 3 | 12 |
| | (25.00) | (50.00) | (8.33) | (25.00) | (100.00) |
| JE | 5 | 8 | 2 | 6 | 18 |
| | (27.78) | (44.44) | (11.11) | (33.33) | (100.00) |
| Lineman | 7 | 18 | 3 | 5 | 30 |
| | (23.33) | (60.00) | (10.00) | (16.67) | (100.00) |
| Meter Reader | 6 | 17 | 1 | 6 | 30 |
| | (20.00) | (56.67) | (3.33) | (20.00) | (100.00) |
| All | 21 | 53 | 9 | 23 | 99 |
| | (21.21) | (53.54) | (9.09) | (23.23) | (100.00) |

*Note*: Figures in parentheses show percentages.
*Source*: Field Survey.

## 3. IMPACT OF EXISTING TARIFF RATES

When asked whether there should be a flat rate system or metered supply to agricultural consumers, a majority of the employees (65 per cent) favoured the flat rate system. This is because the shortage of staff (especially meter readers) and the widely scattered locations of the tube wells make it difficult to monitor the meters. In fact, one of the XENs in Amritsar suggested the flat rate system for domestic supply also to check theft of power. However, one-third of the employees (34 per cent) favoured metered supply to agricultural consumers.

When asked whether the tariff rates should be the same or different, a very large number of employees (85 per cent) favoured different rates for different categories of consumers rather than the same rates for all categories. They were found to be aware of the fact that electricity was put to different uses by different categories of consum-

TABLE 5.17: CHECKING BY THE STAFF TO CONTAIN THEFT OF POWER

| Category of Employee | Frequent Checking | Random Checking | Both Frequent & Random Checking | Total Respondents |
|---|---|---|---|---|
| SE | 1 | 1 | 2 | 3 |
| | (33.33) | (33.33) | (66.67) | (100.00) |
| XEN | 2 | 2 | 2 | 6 |
| | (33.33) | (33.33) | (33.33) | (100.00) |
| SDO | 3 | 4 | 9 | 12 |
| | (25.00) | (33.33) | (75.00) | (100.00) |
| JE | 8 | 10 | 7 | 18 |
| | (44.44) | (55.56) | (38.89) | (100.00) |
| Lineman | 19 | 16 | 10 | 30 |
| | (63.33) | (53.33) | (33.33) | (100.00) |
| Meter Reader | 18 | 18 | 6 | 30 |
| | (60.00) | (60.00) | (20.00) | (100.00) |
| All | 51 | 51 | 36 | 99 |
| | (51.52) | (51.52) | (36.36) | (100.00) |

*Note*: Figures in parentheses show percentages.
*Source*: Field Survey.

ers. Only a few employees (15 per cent) argued in favour of uniform rates.

## 4. EFFICACY OF SUPERVISION, ENFORCEMENT, AND ACCOUNTABILITY

Most of the employees were aware of the existing supervisory and inspecting agencies such as the task force, the flying squad, the vigilance staff, the field staff, etc. They were also aware of the methods followed by these agencies to detect theft of power such as raids, individual official checking, and routine checking by the field staff.

As regards the problems faced by the employees in detecting theft of power (Table 5.18), 69 per cent of them mentioned the problem of the threat of physical harm by individual consumers or groups of individuals. More than half (51 per cent) of the employees mentioned that they faced the problem of political interference in the discharge of their duties, and 33 per cent mentioned the problem of official interference. Only a few employees (9 per cent) did not face any problem.

As regards the incentives given to the employees, almost all of

TABLE 5.18: PROBLEMS FACED BY THE STAFF IN DETECTING THEFT OF POWER

| Category of Employee | Individual/ Collective Threat of Physical Harm | Official Inter-ference | Political Inter-ference | No Problem | Total Respon-dents |
|---|---|---|---|---|---|
| SE | 3 (100.00) | 1 (33.33) | 0 (0.00) | 0 (0.00) | 3 (100.00) |
| XEN | 6 (100.00) | 0 (0.00) | 3 (50.00) | 1 (16.67) | 6 (100.00) |
| SDO | 7 (58.33) | 5 (41.67) | 9 (75.00) | 1 (8.33) | 12 (100.00) |
| JE | 11 (61.11) | 3 (16.67) | 10 (55.56) | 3 (16.67) | 18 (100.00) |
| Lineman | 19 (63.33) | 12 (40.00) | 17 (56.67) | 2 (6.67) | 30 (100.00) |
| Meter Reader | 22 (73.33) | 12 (40.00) | 12 (40.00) | 2 (6.67) | 30 (100.00) |
| All | 68 (68.69) | 33 (33.33) | 51 (51.52) | 9 (9.09) | 99 (100.00) |

*Note*: Figures in parentheses show percentages.
*Source*: Field Survey.

them mentioned that only employees of the task force and the flying squad were given incentives in terms of a fixed percentage (5 per cent) of the detected theft, whereas the field staff was not given any incentive. In fact, the field staff was found to be very unhappy with the board for following this discriminatory policy.

As regards the adequacy of checking by the staff, it was found that the employees were almost evenly divided on this issue. More than half (52 per cent) of the employees regarded checking as adequate, while 45 per cent of them found it to be inadequate.

To improve the functioning of the inspecting and supervising agencies (Table 5.19), 47 per cent of the employees suggested an increase in the frequency of checking, 29 per cent suggested providing better security to the employees against physical violence, 28 per cent suggested stopping of all types of outside interference, and 24 per cent suggested that more incentives should be given to the employees. However, 14 per cent of the employees were satisfied with the present functioning of these agencies.

Regarding the nature of harassment faced by the employees when

TABLE 5.19: IMPROVEMENTS IN THE FUNCTIONING OF SUPERVISION AND INSPECTION AGENCIES

| Category of Employee | More Incentives | Stop Outside Interference | Increase Security agaisnt Physical Violence | Increase Frequency of Checking | Changes in Organizational Structures | No Need, they are Functioning Well | Total Respondents |
|---|---|---|---|---|---|---|---|
| SE | 0 | 0 | 1 | 0 | 0 | 2 | 3 |
| | (0.00) | (0.00) | (33.33) | (0.00) | (0.00) | (66.67) | (100.00) |
| XEN | 2 | 0 | 3 | 3 | 0 | 2 | 6 |
| | (33.33) | (0.00) | (50.00) | (50.00) | (0.00) | (33.33) | (100.00) |
| SDO | 2 | 6 | 2 | 7 | 3 | 1 | 12 |
| | (16.67) | (50.00) | (16.67) | (58.33) | (25.00) | (8.33) | (100.00) |
| JE | 6 | 4 | 4 | 9 | 0 | 3 | 18 |
| | (33.33) | (22.22) | (22.22) | (50.00) | (0.00) | (16.67) | (100.00) |
| Lineman | 8 | 7 | 11 | 13 | 4 | 4 | 30 |
| | (26.67) | (23.33) | (36.67) | (43.33) | (13.33) | (13.33) | (100.00) |
| Meter Reader | 6 | 11 | 8 | 15 | 3 | 2 | 30 |
| | (20.00) | (36.67) | (26.67) | (50.00) | (10.00) | (6.67) | (100.00) |
| All | 24 | 28 | 29 | 47 | 10 | 14 | 99 |
| | (24.24) | (28.28) | (29.29) | (47.47) | (10.10) | (14.14) | (100.00) |

*Note*: Figures in parentheses show percentages.
*Source*: Field Survey.

they did not yield to pressures and reported the pilferage, the employees gave varied responses. About 54 per cent of them mentioned that they suffered from a sense of insecurity due to the threat of being transferred. Another 51 per cent of the employees feared petty harassment by higher officials. Another 15 per cent of the employees mentioned the spoiling of their ACRs by the higher officials. Only 21 per cent of the employees believed that they would not have to face any harassment.

As regards the adequacy of the existing penal system, a majority of the employees (60 per cent) felt that the existing penal system was adequate but that it needed strict enforcement. About 40 per cent of them felt that it was not adequate and that harsher punishment should be introduced.

The employees were asked what steps should be taken to make the employees more accountable regarding their responsibility to improve the quality of service and the detection of pilferage. Their suggestions are given in Table 5.20. An overwhelmingly large

TABLE 5.20: STEPS TO INCREASE ACCOUNTABILITY OF EMPLOYEES

| Category of Employee | Strict Supervision be Enforced Over Staff | Responsibility of each Category of Employees be Fixed | General Motivational Campaign | Any other (Facilities, Incentives, etc.) | Total Respondents |
|---|---|---|---|---|---|
| SE | 2 (66.67) | 3 (100.00) | 1 (33.33) | 0 (0.00) | 3 (100.00) |
| XEN | 5 (83.33) | 3 (50.00) | 0 (0.00) | 2 (33.33) | 6 (100.00) |
| SDO | 10 (83.33) | 8 (66.67) | 3 (25.00) | 1 (8.33) | 12 (100.00) |
| JE | 12 (66.67) | 9 (50.00) | 2 (11.11) | 3 (16.67) | 18 (100.00) |
| Lineman | 21 (70.00) | 10 (33.33) | 4 (13.33) | 12 (40.00) | 30 (100.00) |
| Meter Reader | 20 (66.67) | 13 (43.33) | 4 (13.33) | 7 (23.33) | 30 (100.00) |
| All | 70 (70.71) | 46 (46.46) | 14 (14.14) | 25 (25.25) | 99 (100.00) |

*Note*: Figures in parentheses show percentages.
*Source*: Field Survey.

number of employees (71 per cent) suggested the enforcement of strict supervision over the staff. They included 67 per cent of the SEs, 83 per cent of the XENs, 83 per cent of the SDOs, 67 per cent of the JEs, 70 per cent of the linemen, and 67 per cent of the meter readers. Another important step, suggested by about 46 per cent of the employees, was to establish a clear demarcation of the responsibilities of each category of employees. Other steps related to the provision of better facilities, materials, etc., to the employees (25 per cent) and the adoption of a general motivational campaign (14 per cent).

Table 5.21 shows the perceptions of the employees regarding the punishment to be given for committing theft of power. A majority of the employees (70 per cent) recommended a monetary fine. They included 67 per cent of the SEs, 50 per cent of the XENs, 58 per cent of the SDOs, 67 per cent of the JEs, 70 per cent of the linemen, and 80 per cent of the meter readers. Another 40 per cent of the emplo-yees recommended the disconnection of the power supply as punishment. About one-third of the employees recommended imprisonment. Other punishments which were suggested included public exposure of the culprits at community meetings (9 per cent), public exposure through the radio and newspapers, etc. (7 per cent), and all of these (5 per cent).

## 5. COMMUNITY-BASED INTERVENTION STRATEGIES

Community-based intervention strategies involve the gram panchayats/ municipal committees and other grassroot-level social organizations in the distribution of power to check theft. When asked whether the gram panchayats or the municipal committees should be involved in the distribution of power, a majority of the employees (69 per cent) did not favour their involvement. The reasons which they gave were: (i) these bodies lack the technical expertise to intervene in such matters, (ii) their involvement would politicize the distribution system.

Similarly, a majority of the employees (75 per cent) were against the involvement of social organizations or groups such as the Rotary Clubs, Gymkhana Clubs, youth clubs, mahila mandals, etc., for the reasons mentioned above. Only about one-third (31 per cent) of the employees favoured their involvement. Of them 13 per cent favoured youth clubs, 9 per cent favoured Rotary Clubs, 6 per cent favoured mahila mandals, and 3 per cent favoured Gymkhana Clubs.

TABLE 5.21: PUNISHMENT FOR COMMITTING THEFT OF POWER

| Category of Employee | Monetary Fine | Disconnections of Supply | Imprisonment | Expose through Public Meetings | Expose through Radio/News-papers | All of These | Total Respondents |
|---|---|---|---|---|---|---|---|
| SE | 2 | 0 | 1 | 0 | 0 | 0 | 3 |
| | (66.67) | (0.00) | (33.33) | (0.00) | (0.00) | (0.00) | (100.00) |
| XEN | 3 | 4 | 3 | 0 | 0 | 0 | 6 |
| | (50.00) | (66.67) | (50.00) | (0.00) | (0.00) | (0.00) | (100.00) |
| SDO | 7 | 5 | 4 | 2 | 2 | 1 | 12 |
| | (58.33) | (41.67) | (33.33) | (16.67) | (16.67) | (8.33) | (100.00) |
| JE | 12 | 8 | 2 | 4 | 3 | 0 | 18 |
| | (66.67) | (44.44) | (11.11) | (22.22) | (16.67) | 0.00 | (100.00) |
| Lineman | 21 | 19 | 10 | 1 | 0 | 3 | 30 |
| | (70.00) | (63.33) | (33.33) | (3.33) | (0.00) | (10.00) | (100.00) |
| Meter Reader | 24 | 10 | 12 | 2 | 2 | 1 | 30 |
| | (80.00) | (33.33) | (40.00) | (6.67) | (6.67) | (3.33) | (100.00) |
| All | 69 | 46 | 32 | 9 | 7 | 5 | 99 |
| | (69.70) | (46.46) | (32.32) | (9.09) | (7.07) | (5.05) | (100.00) |

*Note*: Figures in parentheses show percentages.
*Source*: Field Survey.

## 6. INCENTIVES, EMPLOYEES' UNIONS, AND MOTIVATIONAL STEPS

Table 5.22 shows the perceptions of the employees regarding the incentives that may be offered to the employees to make them more interested in their duties, particularly in detecting the theft of power. As is clear from the table, a majority of the employees (55 per cent) suggested that they should be given monetary incentives in the form of lump sum payments or prizes. About 47 per cent of the employees suggested that a fixed percentage of the revenue realized from the detected pilferage should be given to them as is given to the enforcement staff. About 38 per cent of the employees indicated that they should be given more promotions. Very few employees (20 per cent) wanted letters of appreciation as incentives. Thus, monetary incentives emerged as the main motivating factor.

TABLE 5.22: NATURE OF INCENTIVES TO THE EMPLOYEES

| Category of Employee | Letter of Appreciation | Monetary Incentives/ Lump sum Prize | Fixed % of Revenue Realized from Detected Theft be given | Special Incentives be given | Total Respondents |
|---|---|---|---|---|---|
| SE | 0 | 2 | 3 | 0 | 3 |
| | 0.00 | (66.67) | (100.00) | 0.00 | (100.00) |
| XEN | 0 | 4 | 2 | 0 | 6 |
| | 0.00 | (66.67) | (33.33) | 0.00 | (100.00) |
| SDO | 4 | 7 | 6 | 2 | 12 |
| | (33.33) | (58.33) | (50.00) | (16.67) | (100.00) |
| JE | 8 | 10 | 6 | 3 | 18 |
| | (44.44) | (55.56) | (33.33) | (16.67) | (100.00) |
| Lineman | 4 | 19 | 13 | 4 | 30 |
| | (13.33) | (63.33) | (43.33) | (13.33) | (100.00) |
| Meter Reader | 4 | 12 | 17 | 6 | 30 |
| | (13.33) | (40.00) | (56.67) | (20.00) | (100.00) |
| ALL | 20 | 54 | 47 | 15 | 99 |
| | (20.20) | (54.55) | (47.47) | (15.15) | (100.00) |

*Note*: Figures in parentheses show percentages.
*Source*: Field Survey.

The employees were asked about the organizational structure of the PSEB, i.e. whether the present structure should be continued or whether it should be privatized (Table 5.23). The privatization of the PSEB was not favoured by most of the employees. Less than one-half of the employees (46 per cent) favoured privatization. About one-half of the employees (49 per cent) were against privatization for fear of losing their jobs. Only 4 per cent of them did not know whether privatization would help in preventing the theft of power. When further asked whether privatization should be of generation, transmission or distribution, 13 per cent of the employees were in favour of total privatization, while 26 per cent, 6 per cent, and 3 per cent of the employees favoured privatization of distribution, transmission, and generation respectively.

When asked whether power theft was good or bad, almost all the employees, irrespective of their category, claimed to regard the theft of power as a bad practice and condemned it outright. However, they differed on what was bad about it. A very large majority of the employees, about 93 per cent, felt that power theft led to overloading which in turn adversely affected the quality of the supply of electric-

TABLE 5.23: PRIVATIZATION OF PSEB

| Category of Employee | Privatized | Not Privatized | Don't Know | Total Respondents |
|---|---|---|---|---|
| SE | 2 | 1 | 0 | 3 |
| | (66.67) | (33.33) | (0.00) | (0.00) |
| XEN | 5 | 1 | 0 | 6 |
| | (83.33) | (16.67) | (0.00) | (0.00) |
| SDO | 5 | 5 | 2 | 12 |
| | (41.67) | (41.67) | (16.67) | (100.00) |
| JE | 10 | 8 | 0 | 18 |
| | (55.56) | (44.44) | (0.00) | (0.00) |
| Lineman | 10 | 20 | 0 | 30 |
| | (33.33) | (66.67) | (0.00) | (0.00) |
| Meter Reader | 14 | 14 | 2 | 30 |
| | | | (0.00) | (0.00) |
| All | 46 | 49 | 4 | 99 |
| | (46.46) | (49.49) | (4.04) | (100.00) |

*Note*: Figures in parentheses show percentages.
*Source*: Field Survey.

ity. About 76 per cent of the employees felt that it caused financial loss to the PSEB and hence starved it of investible funds to improve the quality of the service to the consumers.

The employees were asked whether a publicity campaign against the evil of power theft should be launched through the media and other means. An overwhelmingly large number of employees (91 per cent) felt that slogans against power theft should be popularized through TV, radio, press, posters, etc., which would be effective in creating mass awareness about the ill effects of power theft. Only 4 per cent of the employees felt that slogans would prove ineffective.

As part of the communication strategy of checking power theft, the employees were asked about the effective ways of communicating with the consumers. Table 5.24 shows the details of their responses. Public meetings (60 per cent) emerged as the most effective way, followed by TV and radio programmes (47 per cent), street plays (33 per cent), and advertisements in the press (26 per cent).

The employees were asked what role the employees' unions could play in checking the theft of power. A majority of the employees (51 per cent) mentioned that the employees' unions could play an important role in checking the theft of power, especially by creating awareness among the masses regarding the bad effects of power theft. However, 46 per cent of the employees were of the view that these unions had no role in checking the theft of power, as they were preoccupied with their own problems. Only 3 per cent of the employees did not comment.

In the course of our survey, we found that the employees were hampered in their duties by a lack of adequate powers which was a serious constraint in making the checking more effective. Due to this constraint, the employees concerned were unable to take suitable and prompt action against the culprits. Accordingly, 72 per cent of the employees suggested that judicial powers (such as the power to arrest, etc.) should be given to the employees from the JE onwards. However, 28 per cent of the employees felt that no additional power should be given to the employees because such powers are misused.

In order to motivate the employees to work more effectively, they may be given incentives, both monetary and non-monetary. In our survey (Table 5.25), a majority of the employees (58 per cent) suggested that they should be given incentives, especially monetary. (This has already been pointed out earlier.) About 43 per cent of the

TABLE 5.24: EFFECTIVE WAYS OF COMMUNICATING WITH CONSUMERS

| Category of Employee | Public Meetings | Ads in the Print Media | TV/Radio Programmes | Street Plays | All of These | Total Respondents |
|---|---|---|---|---|---|---|
| SE | 3 | 1 | 3 | 2 | 0 | 3 |
| | (100.00) | (33.33) | (100.00) | (66.67) | (0.00) | (100.00) |
| XEN | 4 | 2 | 4 | 0 | 1 | 6 |
| | (66.67) | (33.33) | (66.67) | 0.00 | (16.67) | (100.00) |
| SDO | 7 | 4 | 6 | 3 | 4 | 12 |
| | (58.33) | (33.33) | (50.00) | (25.00) | (33.33) | (100.00) |
| JE | 12 | 3 | 4 | 9 | 4 | 18 |
| | (66.67) | (16.67) | (22.22) | (50.00) | (22.22) | (100.00) |
| Lineman | 15 | 7 | 14 | 9 | 9 | 30 |
| | (50.00) | (23.33) | (46.67) | (30.00) | (30.00) | (100.00) |
| Meter Reader | 17 | 7 | 16 | 10 | 8 | 30 |
| | (56.67) | (23.33) | (53.33) | (33.33) | (26.67) | (100.00) |
| All | 58 | 24 | 47 | 33 | 26 | 99 |
| | (58.59) | (24.24) | (47.47) | (33.33) | (26.26) | (100.00) |

*Note*: Figures in parentheses show percentages.
*Source*: Field Survey.

TABLE 5.25: MOTIVATION TO EMPLOYEES TO WORK MORE EFFECTIVELY

| Category of Employee | Incentives | Promotions | Increments Programmes | All of These | Any other (Facilities, etc.) | Total Respondents |
|---|---|---|---|---|---|---|
| SE | 3 | 1 | 0 | 0 | 0 | 3 |
| | (100.00) | (33.33) | (0.00) | (0.00) | (0.00) | (100.00) |
| XEN | 1 | 0 | 0 | 2 | 3 | 6 |
| | (16.67) | (0.00) | (0.00) | (33.33) | (50.00) | (100.00) |
| SDO | 7 | 3 | 3 | 3 | 0 | 12 |
| | (58.33) | (25.00) | (25.00) | (25.00) | (0.00) | (100.00) |
| JE | 14 | 11 | 4 | 2 | 4 | 18 |
| | (77.78) | (61.11) | (22.22) | (11.11) | (22.22) | (100.00) |
| Lineman | 16 | 12 | 4 | 11 | 5 | 30 |
| | (53.33) | (40.00) | (13.33) | (36.67) | (16.67) | (100.00) |
| Meter Reader | 17 | 16 | 8 | 9 | 3 | 30 |
| | (56.67) | (53.33) | (26.67) | (30.00) | (10.00) | (100.00) |
| All | 58 | 43 | 19 | 27 | 15 | 99 |
| | (58.59) | (43.43) | (19.19) | (27.27) | (15.15) | (100.00) |

*Note*: Figures in parentheses show percentages.
*Source*: Field Survey.

TABLE 5.26: TECHNICAL AND MOTIVATIONAL TRAINING TO THE EMPLOYEES

| Category of Employee | Special Training should be given | Increase Social Awareness | No Need for Training | Total Respondents |
|---|---|---|---|---|
| SE | 3 (100.00) | 1 (33.33) | 0 (0.00) | 3 (100.00) |
| XEN | 5 (83.33) | 0 (0.00) | 3 (50.00) | 6 (100.00) |
| SDO | 10 (83.33) | 1 (8.33) | 2 (16.67) | 12 (100.00) |
| JE | 15 (83.33) | 5 (27.78) | 2 (11.11) | 18 (100.00) |
| Lineman | 24 (80.00) | 6 (20.00) | 5 (16.67) | 30 (100.00) |
| Meter Reader | 21 (70.00) | 9 (30.00) | 5 (16.67) | 30 (100.00) |
| All | 78 (78.79) | 22 (22.22) | 17 (17.17) | 99 (100.00) |

*Note*: Figures in parentheses show percentages.
*Source*: Field Survey.

employees suggested that more promotional avenues should be opened to them. Anohter 19 per cent of them wanted that special increments should be given. Another 27 per cent of the employees wanted all of these incentives. Only 15 per cent of the employees wanted other kinds of motivation such as better facilities and good working environment, etc.

As regards the type of training to be given to the employees, the employees reacted positively to suggestions of technical and motivational training, as is clear from Table 5.26. A large majority (79 per cent) of them suggested that special training should be given to the employees, especially in relation to checking the theft of power. They included all the SEs, 83 per cent each of the XENs, SDOs, and JEs, 80 per cent of the linemen, and 70 per cent of the meter readers. Training related to increasing social awareness was suggested by 22 per cent of the employees. However, 17 per cent of the employees felt that there was no need for any training as the employees were already trained.

The following conclusions emerge from the analysis of the perceptions of the employees.

1. The Major problems faced by the employees in the distribution system were the shortage of maintenance materials as well as their sub-standard and poor quality. The lower-rank field employees underlined the shortage of tools (T&P). Some respondent employees mentioned lack of incentives and the absence of cooperation from the superior officers. The quality of service was poor because of overloaded transformers, the poor maintenance of the T&D network, and the shortage of maintenance staff.
2. People indulge in theft of power to save money; they steal because they believe the tariff rates are high and the supply is not adequate and also because at times it is difficult to get a connection and long delays are involved. Some people are induced to adopt this malpractice when they see others doing the same thing and suffering no consequences or geting away by offering small bribes. Theft is more pronounced during the night, it occurs almost throughout the year, and perhaps, occurs move often in summer. Industrial consumers indulge more in the theft of power, followed by domestic consumers.
3. People of all (without exception) social backgrounds indulge in power theft to some degree; educated people indulge in it more than the illiterate people. Politically influential people are more involved in pilferage than others.
4. People waste energy through the unnecessary use of power, the use of high wattage appliances, and due to ignorance of energy-efficient appliances and energy conservation methods.
5. An overwhelming number of employees agreed that pilferage was done with the connivance of the employees, perhaps at all levels.
6. Tampering with meters, use of *kundis*/direct supply, and use of defective meters are the main methods of pilfering power. Sealing of meters should be improved, defective meters should be replaced quickly, naked joints on the main lines should be sealed, and, if possible, all the meters in a village should be installed at one place.
7. It will be helpful to create social awareness regarding the implications of the theft of power particularly as these relate to the quality of the service as well as the resultant higher price to be charged from honest consumers. Guilty persons should be punished and exposed in public.
8. The majority of the employees believed that a reduction in tariff would be helpful. However, a significant section of the employees

was of the opinion that the level of tariff was not as important a factor as the quality of service to the consumers. A significant section of the employees suggested that the minimum monthly charges should be increased, as this step would discourage the tendency to steal power. A large majority of the employees believed that the tube wells were widely scattered and that there was inadequate staff to conduct effective metering. However, one-third of the employees favoured different tariff rates for different categories of consumers.

9. A large section of the employees was scared of individual as well as collective hostility and feared threats of physical violence from evil-minded and influential consumers. Political and official interference was also a significant factor, and the employees feared harassment of various types such as transfers, spoiling of their ACRs, etc.
10. Like the consumers, the employees were found to be sceptical about involving community-based grassroot-level organizations such as the gram panchayats and the municipal committees in the distribution of power. They believed that these bodies lacked the expertise and, being political in nature, they would jeopardize the distribution system. Similarly, the employees were not enthusiastic about involving other social organizations or groups such as youth clubs, mahila mandals, and Rotary Clubs, etc., in the distribution of power.
11. Frequent and surprise checking would be quite effective anti-theft measures. The field staff strongly felt that they should also be given monetary rewards similar to the ones given to the enforcement staff. Lump sum cash prizes, promotions, and social recognition would provide them with strong motivational incentives.
12. Employees were evenly divided over the issue of the privatization of the Punjab State Electricity Board, especially due to the fear of losing their jobs. However, a significant section of the employees was of the opinion that privatization of distribution would be helpful in reducing the pilferage of power.
13. Officers generally complained of inadequate powers to punish the culprits. They wanted judicial powers for the quick dispensation of punishment such as the power to impose fines, etc.
14. Almost everybody considered power theft to be a bad practice. It adversely affected efficiency, reduced motivation, overloaded the

T&D system, decreased the quality of service, and increased the financial losses of the PSEB.

15. The employees generally favoured technical as well as motivational training to deal with the problems of the pilferage of power. They favoured mass campaigns to increase social awareness through public meetings, TV and radio, advertisements and hoardings, etc.

CHAPTER 6

# Summary and Policy Recommendations

The establishment of basic and heavy industries in the public sector was one of the basic planks of the planned economic development strategy adopted in India on the eve of independence. The Mahalanobis model of development provided the theoretical basis for the path of self-reliant development. The process of economic development dramatically incresed the demand for electric power in India. In response, the electric power system has expanded at a phenomenal rate of nearly 9 per cent per annum over the last fifty years. However, the demand continues to outstrip the supply. To ensure an adequate supply of electricity, huge amounts of physical and financial resources are required. From the long-term perspective, it appears that the existing pattern of energy use is not sustainable. It warrants a highly efficient use of energy resources in general and of electric power in particular. Energy service needs to be improved by encouraging the use of energy-efficient appliances, through the implementation of demand-side management, the adoption of energy conservation methods, and the minimization of electricity dissipation and wastage in the process of supplying electricity to consumers. Thus, the issues related to the conservation of energy and its efficient use in high-priority areas warrants our immediate attention.

The State Electricity Boards that are primarily responsible for the management of the major part of the generation, transmission, and distribution of electric power in India are plagued with technical inefficiencies and serious financial coustraints. These boards are required to earn a minimum net return of not less than 3 per cent on their average capital base. However, the boards have continued to incur financial losses. Commercial losses without taking the state government's subvention into consideration during 1992–3 in the country as a whole were Rs. 4,560 crore and increased to Rs. 1,3817 crore in 1999–2000. Commercial losses taking the state subsidy into consideration were Rs. 2,725 crore in 1992–3 and they increased to Rs. 11,682 crore in 1999–2000. In the same years the gross subsidy to the agricultural sector increased from Rs. 7,335 crore to Rs. 22,703 crore and to the domestic sector, it increased from Rs. 2,035 crore to Rs. 8,082 crore respectively. Obviously, such a financial situation cannot continue, as it is not sustainable in the long run.

One of the major reasons for the poor financial performance of the State Electricity Boards in the country has been the high transmission and distribution (T&D) losses, which are officially reported to range from 21 per cent to 26 per cent per annum. Official estimates of T&D losses are at best intelligent guesses, and they conceal more than what they reveal. In fact, the official estimates have become more of a policy decision than the true estimates since a significant part of the T&D losses, including pilferage, may be included in agricultural consumption where electricity is mostly unmetered and is supplied at a flat rate. The actual T&D losses in many states may range from 30 per cent to 50 per cent of the total supply. The internationally accepted norm for T&D losses is 7 per cent to 10 per cent of the total supply. In Indian conditions 12 per cent to 15 per cent is the accepted norm. Therefore, there is a great scope for reduction in the T&D losses.

T&D losses consist of technical and non-technical losses. Technical losses can be reduced but cannot be completely eliminated. Non-technical losses are primarily due to pilferage and theft of power from the transmission and distribution network. Pilferage of power or power theft may be defined as the dishonest use of electricity by a person, including legal consumers, by either bypassing the meter completely or by tampering with the meter in such a way that it does not record consumption fully or even partially. This type of electricity consumption is not billed and paid for. The pilferage of power has a number of consequences. On the one hand, it involves revenue loss to the board and, on the other, it encourages wastage of energy, as there is no motivation to conserve it. If pilferage coincides with peak system demand, it exerts pressure on the existing generation capacity, which requires further additions to the installed capacity to meet the increased demand. Lastly, in addition to the financial losses, pilferage of power has become such a menace that it is seriously eating into the vitals of the administration and management of the SEBs (utilities). If not effectively checked, the employees also get demotivated, and this loss of morale affects the operational efficiency of the utilities and in turn compromises the accountability of the management as well.

To overcome the various problems faced by the electricity supply utilities, the laws governing the supply of electricity in India, namely the Indian Electricity Act, 1910, the Electricity (Supply) Act, 1956, and the Indian Electricity Rules, 1956 were amended in 1990s. The Electricity Laws (Amendment) Act, 1998 and the Electricity Regulatory Commission Act, 1998 provide the framework for the regulation of electricity. They establish new legal, administrative, and financial provisions to allow and encourage private participation in the power sector. Now all the previous laws governing the functioning of electricity industry are being replaced by the Electricity Act passed by the Parliament in May 2003. It has been argued that the problem of pilferage of power has become socially institutionalized and even the best technical and/or administrative measures, including privatization of distribution, may not achieve the desired results. Therefore, the problem has been addressed from the social perspective. In this study, the problems of pilferage of power and inefficient energy conservation practices have been subjected to a systematic analysis. The main objective of the study is to understand the socio-economic dynamics of the problem of the pilferage of electric power and to work out organizational, managerial, motivational, and community-oriented solutions to combat this menace. Such a study is essential to evolve social marketing and communication packages to enlist community support and to generate social awareness regarding power theft and its negative effects on the quality of service. This will also help us to prepare motivational programmes and training modules for the staff of the electricity boards, various consumer groups, and local activists.

To locate the problem of the pilferage of power in its proper perspective, the technical and financial performance of the Punjab State Electricity Board and the erstwhile Haryana State Electricity Board were critically examined and the existing rules and procedures to check pilferage were reviewed. To assess the perceptions of both consumers and employees regarding various aspects of the problem, a questionnaire was administered. A sample of various consumer categories and employees from three districts, namely, Amritsar, Jalandhar, and Rupnagar were selected through a stratified purposive sampling design.

The main findings of the analysis of the financial and technical performances are given below.

- An analysis of the performance of the Punjab State Electricity Board and the erstwhile Haryana State Electricity Board reveals that in the state development plans, electric power development has been accorded a very high priority in terms of the allocation of Plan outlays and the electricity supply system grew at an impressive rate.
- Many factors contributed to the poor technical efficiency, namely, the poor quality of coal having a high ash content, the overloading of transmission and distribution systems due to lack of investment in their expansion, and poor management.
- The financial performance has been poor because of high management and administrative inefficiencies, irrational pricing policies, the state-directed subsidization policy for which the SEBs were not fully compensated, and a complete lack of a commercial outlook.
- Political appointees without any professional background and members of the state bureaucracy occupied the top management positions without any accountability for the performance of the electricity boards.
- No effort was made by the management to achieve the statutory rate of return (ROR) of 3 per cent on the average capital base. No one was held responsible for the violation of the statutes as the political leadership and the top management were in league with each other. However, subsidies were extended to favoured consumers on the directions of the political bosses without the board being compensated for the expense involved. In fact, the continued violation of the statute to ensure the minimum of the 3 per cent rate of return on the average capital base may be characterized as one of the major reasons for landing the SEBs in a state of bankruptcy.
- Another critical factor was the lack of transparency and accountability in the operations of the system. As has been pointed out by the Haryana Electricity Regulatory Commission, without the proper metering of the transmission and distribution systems it is not possible to evaluate the technical performance of the system as a whole. To ensure the efficient functioning of the public enterprises in a democratic country, its operations must be made transparent and accountable. Otherwise, vested interests will take over and behind the curtain corruption may become rampant, and by the time it is exposed it may be too late.

- Haryana is in the process of implementing power sector reforms, which are basically a part of the IMF/World Bank-sponsored structural adjustment programmes. The agenda of the sponsoring multilateral financial institutions does not necessarily coincide with the interests of the state economies. Second, experience teaches us that no reform or institutional change can be successfully accomplished under external pressure. What with almost certainly emerge under these circumstances are half-hearted reforms which may prove even worse than the disease they are meant to cure. The analysis of the tariff orders of the Haryana Electricity Regulatory Commission clearly brings out that pilferage of power needs immediate attention.

The main findings of the study of the perceptions of both consumers and employees are as follows:

- A common perception among most consumers and employees is that people/consumers of almost all socio-economic and educational backgrounds indulge in the pilferage of power. However, consumers having the political backing and the direct or indirect patronage of highly placed officers indulge in this malpractice more than the others. People indulge in pilferage generally with the active connivance, at times passive acquiescence, of the employees.

  Industrialists indulge in power theft at the time of power shortages or otherwise with the active involvement of the employees. Landlords indulge in pilferage as they know that their political clout and the flat rate system offer them a convenient cover. An analysis of the perceptions establishes beyond doubt that the employees, by and large, personally know the consumers who indulge in the pilferage of power.
- People indulge in pilferage to evade paying for the consumption of power and to save money despite having the capacity to pay. They feel tempted to resort to this malpractice when they see others do the same and escape punishment or get away by paying small bribes or fines. Though a majority of the respondents believe that higher tariff rates encourage pilferage, a significant minority is of the opinion that tariff has no bearing on power theft. One of the ways to discourage pilferage is to impose minimum monthly charges per kilowatt of connected load.
- Tampering with the meters, use of *kundies*/direct supply from the lines, and use of defective meters or delayed replacement have

been identified as the major methods of pilfering power. Most of these methods are detectable and are known to the employees at one level or the other. Farmers install heavier motors than the sanctioned load as a matter of routine. They use the agricultural connection for other purposes, and again the flat rate system provides them with a conduit to pilfer power with no additional responsibility to pay for the increased consumption.

- A large section of the employees is actively involved in the pilferage of power or they are silent spectators. As and when they seek to check it, the field staff faces the consumer's hostility, both individual and collective, even to the extent of facing physical assault or a threat to their life, and there are no adequate security measures in place to combat such situations. They also feel insecure due to undue pressure and harassment, such as threats of transfer and the deliberately negative assessments given in the annual confidential reports by their superiors. The employees believe that corruption has been institutionalized to the extent that it has gained social acceptability and represents the path of least resistance. By ignoring pilferage, they keep their superiors in good humour and perhaps in the process make some easy money through bribes. Inaction is the highest form of job security, and obliging the consumer for a consideration is the most rewarding approach to safeguarding professional security.
- On the issue of the privatization of the SEBs, the employees are either reluctant or are evenly divided. The latent fear among them is that some of them may lose their jobs. But a significant section of the employees is of the opinion that the privatization of electricity distribution will help reduce the pilferage of power. It is interesting to note that a majority of the consumers are in favour of the privatization of distribution. In particular, an overwhelming majority of industrial and commercial consumers are strongly in favour of privatization. The reasons put forward are that it will involve less corruption and will improve the quality of service. However, most of the consumers do not understand the implications of privatization in all its aspects.
- Consumers as well as employees are generally sceptical about the involvement of community-based organizations such as the gram panchayats and municipal committees. They believe that these institutions have not been functioning with the required sense of responsibility, are faction ridden, and that they will be sectarian

and not quite judicious in their approach. The respondents are not even enthusiastic about involving other social organizations such as youth clubs, mahila mandals, Rotary Clubs, etc. This cynicism towards local self-government bodies stems from the ways in which the panchayats and the municipal committees have been conducting themselves in other spheres of social and public life.

- Most of the consumers and employees believe that the energy-use pattern of consumers is wasteful. They often indulge in the unnecessary use of power. Consumers use appliances of higher wattage; in fact, they are not even conscious of its negative implications. Some consumers waste power by showing off at public ceremonies such as weddings and parties. Very few consumers are aware of energy-efficient alternative appliances, the monetary benefits of saving energy by way of reducing their electricity bills, and the social significance of the conservation of energy.
- Most of the consumers and employees agree that the theft of power is a bad practice and should be discouraged and the culprits exposed in public. Steps should be taken to increase the awareness of the people regarding the effects of pilferage on the quality of the service, its impact on tariff, as well as the impact on further investment to improve electricity supply, etc. The respondents strongly favoured various publicity methods to highlight the evil effects of power theft. They have suggested that public meetings should be held and that the people should be directly involved in decision-making which will give them a sense of participation and increase their moral commitment to discourage this evil practice. This will discredit the culprits in the eyes of the public and will discourage them in the future. Publicity through radio and television has been identified as the other important channel for increasing public awareness.
- It has been noted that the existing laws to deal with the pilferage of power are many but their enforcement has been quite weak. However, the officers generally complain of having inadequate powers to punish the guilty. They even want judicial powers for quick dispensation of punishment. The employees want additional incentives and rewards for apprehending the culprits. Employees generally favour technical as well as motivational training to deal with the problem of the theft of power.
- Most of the consumers do not recognize the theft of power in the agricultural sector, though they prefer the metered supply to the

flat rate system. However, the agricultural consumers are strongly in favour of the flat rate system. A majority of the employees also favours the flat rate system for agricultural consumers as tube-wells are scattered and the staff is inadequate to meet the requirements of effective metering. The respondents are generally in favour of a subsidized supply of electricity to the agricultural sector.

The case for adopting unmetered supply at a flat rate instead of a metered supply needs to be carefully examined. The system of unmetered supply at flat rates was introduced when tube-wells were few in number, they were widely scattered, and the consumption per tube-well was relatively small. Large staffs were required for meter reading and to keep an effective check on the tampering of meters, to prevent power pilferage, and to ensure the maintenance of meters, etc. Under these conditions, the flat rate system was considered to be a cost effective and administratively convenient method of charging for electricity supply. Over a period of time, however, the landlords as well as the officials of the SEBs have developed a vested interest in maintaining the flat rate system.

For the landlords, it is convenient because there is no check on the amount of power consumed or wasted, there is no threat of punishment if they install motors of higher capacity than the sanctioned load, and there is no effective check on other electrical equipment being used. For the SEB's officials, it is convenient because it avoids the headache of monitoring the consumers who are widely scattered, who are politically influential, and who can create problems for them. For the management also, it is quite easy to administer. The flat rate system has become an easy cover to escape accountability to improve the efficiency of the transmission and distribution system as it makes it difficult to have a precise estimate of the technical losses. It has been noted that the electricity boards transfer a significant part of the T&D losses to the agricultural consumption account, making it difficult to assess the extent of the pilferage of power. As agricultural supply is highly subsidized, financial losses are not taken seriously. In fact, the flat rate system has become a den of corruption and has led to the non-accountability of the SEBs as well as the agricultural consumers. The landlords are politically influential since they control village vote banks and no political party in power can afford to displease them. Thus, the cure has become worse than the disease. However, if the administrative as well as the financial health of the SEBs is to be restored, the flat rate system shall have to be dispensed with immediately. In Punjab, to honour its election promise, the elected Akali Dal government abolished the flat rate system of tariff with effect from 1997–8 and replaced it with unmetered free supply. Under these circumstances, it is not possible to evaluate the technical performance of the transmission and distribution system.

Before making specific policy recommendations, we should examine the underlying reasons behind the behaviour patterns and responses of the consumers and the employees. The key motive behind the pilferage of power is stated to be the desire to evade the payment for electricity consumption dues, and a further inducement is provided by the lack of punishment for indulging in this malpractice. At the same time, people continue to believe this to be a bad practice. This response pattern needs to be examined in the historical context. The consumers continue to believe that electricity supply by a public utility is the social responsibility of the state and that the government should bear the cost as it does with social services in the fields of education, health, etc.

Second, the general attitude towards the services or goods provided by the state is rather casual due to the low level of democratic and social consciousness and lack of social commitment. If a businessman supplies the same commodity, it is considered legitimate for him to earn a profit but the people's expectations from the government are different. The government is expected to supply electricity free or at a subsidized rate. In the community/neighbourhood people do not muster the required moral courage to prevent one another from indulging in socially undesirable and illegitimate practices. Collective efforts as well as the moral courage to condemn socially undesirable practices are rather weak. Campaigns need to be launched to increase social consciousness and social accountability. The people should be made to realize that the supply of public services or goods involves a cost, which must ultimately be borne by society. People should be made to appreciate the fact that electricity is a precious source of energy, and that its supply is a commercial proposition. They should be encouraged to use it optimally and pay for their consumption. Such a change in the attitude of the people can be brought about through awareness campaigns and various strategies of social marketing.

The employees of the public enterprises in general and of the public utilities in particular also suffer from the lack of social consciousness and social commitment which marks the society at large. Their attitude towards public enterprises is quite different from that of the employees of private enterprises. The required work culture and professional ethics need to be inculcated among the employees of public utilities. Training modules may be prepared to increase their social consciousness and to enhance their professional skills and commitment.

It has been noted that consumers as well as employees are generally sceptical about the involvement of community-based organizations as well as local self-government bodies such as gram panchayats and municipal committees in the distribution of power. Their response pattern is perfectly valid in the light of their past experience regarding the functioning of these institutions. However, in a democratic country, they must be made to succeed. The major reason for the failure of these institutions is the lack of democratic consciousness and the lack of will to participate in efforts to rectify the deficiencies. Therefore, steps should be taken to generate the required social consciousness to make these institutions effective, purposeful, and accountable.

A technical solution to the problem of the pilferage of power no matter how foolproof it may be in theory will prove inadequate unless the system is made transparent and all the stakeholders are involved in the decision-making process. To achieve this goal, the vested interests of the people who control the present set up will have to be exposed in order to weaken their resistance to reforming the system and to ensure that the new reforms deliver the desired results. It is already being reported that in some regions where the SEBs have tried to install meters or where employees go for revenue collection, there is a high degree of resistance from the villagers. At times, it turns into a law and order problem. Unfortunately, most of the dominant political parties when in the opposition adopt populist slogans like free supply of electricity to agriculture, launch campaigns not to pay electricity bills with a promise that 'if they come to power, bills will be waived off', etc. This politically opportunistic attitude undermines and weakness the social ethos and provides legitimacy to irresponsible social behaviour. In such a situation, it becomes very difficult for these political parties to evolve an accountable system when they do come to power. The electricity pricing policy needs to be depoliticized. Therefore, social awareness campaigns and social marketing have become essential.

In the light of the observations made above, we shall work out socially relevant policy packages and devise intervention strategies.

## POLICY RECOMMENDATIONS

### 1. *Organizational Changes*

At present, in most of the states the entire electric power system, i.e. generation, transmission, and distribution, is administered by a single corporate authority, the State Electricity Board. The SEBs need to be restructured to make them more responsive and efficient. It is absolutely clear that the boards cannot be run like state government departments. They must develop a commercial outlook.

In some of the states, power sector reforms are in the process of being implemented. The generation, the transmission, and the distribution functions have been separated and entrusted to different companies. In the field of power generation and distribution, private and foreign companies are being invited to participate. State Electricity Regulatory Commissions are being established to regulate the electric power supply business in the states. This is primarily the World Bank model which is being introduced. Credit-starved state governments are implementing these reforms to be eligible for multilateral borrowings. The states that have opted for this model are finding it politically as well as financially difficult to honour the terms and conditions of borrowings from the World Bank.

The other alternative is to restructure the SEBs by providing relative autonomy to the generation, transmission, and distribution systems. Their working should be made transparent and accountable. A number of alternative organizational structures are being debated these days. However, as far as the problem of pilferage is concerned, organizational changes *per se* cannot eradicate the problem. The pilferage of power has been highly institutionalized. The mindset of the people needs to be changed, for which the involvement of people and social organizations as well as local self-government bodies in the distribution of electricity will need to be solicited. The local self-government bodies may be provided with incentives like a share in the revenue realized for their development work. This will make the management of the distribution system participatory, ensure more accountability, and make it more responsive. The privatization of the generation and distribution systems *per se* may not solve the problem. It may amount to the abdication of social responsibility on the part of the SEBs, which may have serious consequences for the poor consumers.

The experience of restructuring in Haryana reveals that the management of all the generation, transmission, and distribution companies is autonomous only on paper. The political leadership in power exercised through bureaucrats of the administrative services controls the newly created corporations. In fact, in the erstwhile HSEB, there was only one senior IAS officer as a chairman of the board; now four new posts of managing directors have been created and the state bureaucrats who may not know even the difference between watt and voltage have occupied them. It is essential that in the restructured corporations, management professionals should be appointed as chief executives and should be provided with autonomy of action and should be made accountable for the results. Otherwise, restructuring by itself will not achieve much. It is recommended that the generation, transmission, and the distribution systems be made autonomous. Management must be made transparent and accountable for its performance.

2. *Management Practices*

(i) The first task to be performed by the SEBs is to make its energy accounting systems transparent. Energy audits should be introduced at the district or any other technically feasible administrative level. Let each executive engineer account for the total supply, sale of electricity, and revenue realized in his or her division. T&D losses at the district level should be made public. Let the people know which regions and which groups of consumers indulge in the pilferage of power.

(ii) To obtain a more precise estimate of the T&D losses, no consumer should be allowed unmetered supply. To reduce the scope of the pilferage of power and the inefficient use of energy and also to increase accountability, all agricultural consumers should be provided with metered supply. Initially supply may be metered and agricultural consumers may be given an option of paying at a flat rate or according to metered consumption. It is appreciated that a switch over from the flat rate or from free supply to metered supply is going to be a politically sensitive decision and that there will be resistance from the landlords as well as from the officials of the boards who have developed a vested interest in the continuance of the system. However, the mass media, including newspapers, radio, and television, should be utilized to highlight the drawbacks of unmetered supply. Let there be a public debate on the issue.

3. *Technical Solutions*

An assessment of technical solutions to the problem of power theft has not been attempted in this study. However, it is recommended that the available techniques to make tampering more difficult—by introducing electronic meters and tamper-proof boxes for meters, effective sealing of meters with numbered paper seals, installing meters at one point in a village/locality, etc.—may be adopted.

4. *Administrative Measures*

(i) It has been noted that even the norms of regular and frequent checking laid down by the SEBs are not being strictly followed. Regular and random checking schedules should be strictly followed. The vigilance department should be strengthened and flying squads should be made to function effectively.

(ii) Responsibilities of the field staff, meter readers, linemen, junior engineers, SDOs, etc., should be clearly demarcated and the accountability of each should be fixed. Employees discharging their responsibilities efficiently should be identified and given incentives such as extra increments, cash prizes, merit certificates, etc.

(iii) To break the nexus between the unscrupulous consumers and the corrupt employees, the transfer policy should be made rational. If the functioning of the management is made transparent, and the erring officials are dealt with strictly according to the law, it will encourage conscientious employees to improve their efficiency. Regular meetings with the field staff, and the quick redressal of their genuine grievances coupled with motivational strategies to improve morale will go a long way to change the work culture.

5. *Motivational Measures*

(i) It has been observed that people indulge in the pilferage of power to escape having to pay for their consumption, that people regard the goods and services provided by the public utilities as free and that there is a lack of social commitment and responsibility that needs to be inculcated and developed. This warrants a change in the attitude of the people towards the evil of power theft, for which creative interventions are required.

(ii) Consumers need to be educated about the fact that public (government) service is not a free service, and that it is the people collectively who ultimately pay for the irresponsible behaviour of an individual consumer. Therefore, it is in the personal (private) interest of an individual to intervene if somebody indulges in wrongful social behaviour. People should be educated about the ethical, social, and financial losses which result because of the actions of certain individuals, i.e. if due to pilferage or some other reason, the electricity system becomes overloaded and the transformer is burnt out, the whole neighbourhood has to suffer from darkness, inconvenience, and discomfort. An awareness campaign should be launched to increase social accountability among the people by making them aware of the implications of such behaviour. People should be informed:

(a) of the replacement cost of the transformers which ultimately will have to be borne by the consumers collectively;
(b) of the inconvenience caused to the consumers and the production losses which result due to the unavailability of electricity till the transformer is replaced;
(c) overloading of the system may lead to a drop in voltage, which may damage the electrical appliances in homes or at farms;
(d) accidents due to pilferage can be fatal.

(iii) The supervision of the distribution system may be entrusted collectively to the gram panchayat and the officials of the SEB to ensure that the distribution system functions satisfactorily. The villagers, along with the SEB staff at the local level, should be involved, incentives provided, and accountability fixed, i.e. if a transformer is burnt out due to overloading, the local official of the electricity board and the gram panchayat should be held jointly responsible for this. The following procedure may be introduced:

(a) The concerned lineman may be asked to specify the reasons for the burning out of the transformer.
(b) The panchayat should also be asked to hold a meeting of the gram sabha, which may discuss the issue and submit its views on the possible reasons for the damage to the transformer. The gram sabha may be asked to suggest measures to check the recurreuce of this type of incident. The basic idea remains to involve the community and to engender a sense of participation among the local people in the events of their neighbourhood.
(c) Block or district level joint committees of representatives of the SEBs and the block samiti/zila parishad may be formed to review the reports of the panchayats and to make their recom-

mendations to the state government/the SEB for corrective measures.

(iv) Various studies have established beyond doubt that there is a great potential for the introduction of energy-efficient appliances. It has been reported that by improving the quality of foot-valves, GI sections, and delivery pipes, the power consumption of irrigation pump sets can be reduced by 30 to 35 per cent. A vigorous campaign should be launched to promote energy conservation methods. Even the manufacturers would most probably like to participate in this endeavour.

## INCENTIVES AND PUNITIVE ACTIONS

Three levels of incentives and punitive actions may be introduced:

(A) *Community-Oriented Incentives*

These should include:

(i) Provision for allocating 12.5 per cent more assistance to the first 500 panchayats showing a better performance for establishing independent feeders.

(ii) If there is a reduction in the cost of maintenance or capital cost, half of it should be transferred to the panchayat to improve power supply to the village or for other developmental work.

(iii) Some tube well connections may be provided on the recommendations of the Panchayat, which shows better performance.

(B) *Punitive Actions*

(i) If a transformer is burnt out more than twice in a year, the panchayat will have to bear up to 50 per cent of the replacement cost.

(ii) A lineman with poor performance during his tenure of two years should be given administrative disincentives such as stoppage of increment, warning, transfer, etc.

(C) *Social Marketing Campaign*

The social marketing campaign having two components may be launched:

(i) Training
(ii) Community Awareness Campaign

The basic themes of the campaign would be:

(a) Power pilferage is theft and constitutes a crime as much as house-breaking, picking pockets, etc.
(b) Power theft should not be ignored by the people shrugging it off as 'not my problem', since it directly affects every consumer through low/fluctuating voltage, frequent burning out of bulbs, TV sets, pumps/motors, and other equipment and finally by increased power tariffs.

The proposals described above are illustrative in character and may be modified according to the needs and peculiarities of the local situation. If the above measures are undertaken, they will go a long way to check effectively the menace of power theft in India and will help in restoring the financial health of the SEBs or the publicly owned distribution companies. If such a strategy fails, possible alternatives would be to let the situation drift even further or to privatize.

# References

Ahluwalia, S. Sanjeev, 'Power Tariff Reforms in India', *Economic and Political Weekly*, vol. 35, no. 38, 16–22 Sept. 2000, pp. 3407–19.

Alternative Survey Group, *Alternative Economic Survey*, various issues, 1993 to 2001, New Delhi.

Baijal, Pradip, 'Restructuring Power Sector in India: A Base Paper', *Economic and Political Weekly*, vol. 34, no. 39, 25 Sept.–1 Oct. 1999, pp. 2795–803.

Balu, V., 'Issues and Challenges Concerning Privatization and Regulation in the Power Sector', *Energy for Sustainable Development*, vol. III, Bangalore: IEI, March 1997, pp. 6–13.

Bhaduri, Amit and Deepak Nayyar, *The Intelligent Person's Guide to Liberalisation*, New Delhi: Penguin Books, 1996.

Centre for the Monitoring of Indian Economy, *India's Energy Sector*, Bombay, 1995 and 2001.

Chossudovsky, Michel, *The Globalisation of Poverty: Impact of IMF and World Bank Reforms*, Penang: Third World Network, 1997.

Crew, Michael A. and Paul R. Kleindorfer, *Public Utility Economics*, New York: St. Martin's Press, 1979.

Das, Anjana, Jyoti Parikh and S. Kirit Parikh, '*Power:* The Critical Infrastructure', in *India Development Report 1999–2000*, Mumbai: Kirit S., New Delhi: Oxford University Press, 1999, pp. 113–39.

Das, Anjana and Jyoti Parikh, 'Making Maharashtra State Electricity Board Commercially Viable', *Economic and Political Weekly*, vol. 35, no. 14, 1–6 April 2000, pp. 1201–8.

Economic and Statistical Organization, *Statistical Abstract of Haryana 1998–9*, Planning Department, Government of Haryana, 2000.

Gadgil, Ashok and G. Jannuzzi, 'Conservation Potential of Compact Fluorescent Lamps in India and Brazil', *Energy Policy*, vol. 19, no. 6, 1991 pp. 449–63.

Godbole, Madhav, 'What is Right in Economics is Wrong in Politics', *Economic and Political Weekly*, vol. 33, nos. 42–3, 17–24 October 1998, pp. 2696–7.

Goldenberg, J., et al., *Energy for a Sustainable World*, New Delhi: Wiley Eastern, 1988.

Government of Haryana, The Haryana Electricity Reform Act, *1997, Haryana Government Gazette* (*Extraordinary*), Chandigarh, 10 March 1998.

Government of India, Planning Commission, *The Pricing of Electricity: Report of the Planning Unit of the Indian Statistical Institute (ISI)*, New Delhi, 1962.

Government of India, *Report of the Energy Survey of India Committee*, New Delhi, 1965.

———, *Report of the Fuel Policy Committee*, New Delhi, 1974.

———, *The Electricity (Supply) Act*, 1948, New Delhi, 1996.

———, Central Electricity Authority, *15th Annual Electric Power Survey of India*, New Delhi, 1995.

———, Ministry of Finance, *Economic Survey 2000–1*, New Delhi, 2001.

———, Ministry of Irrigation and Power, *Power Economy Committee, Reports of Various Groups*, New Delhi, 1970.

———, Ministry of Power, *Report of the Committee on Private Sector Participation in Power Distribution* (Coecho Committee Report), 1998.

———, Planning Commission, *Report on the Working of State Electricity Boards and Electricity Departments*, New Delhi, 2000.

———, *Report of the Committee on Power*, New Delhi, 1980.

Government of Punjab, Planning Department, *Statistical Abstract of Punjab*, various yearly issues, Chandigarh.

Gulati, Ashok and Sudha Narayanan, 'Demystifying Fertiliser and Power Subsidies in India', *Economic and Political Weekly*, vol. 35, no. 10, 4–10 March 2000, pp. 784–94.

Haryana Electricity Regulatory Commission, *Commission's Order on Annual Revenue Requirement for Transmission and Bulk Supply Business for 2000–1*, and *Transmission and Bulk Supply Tariff*, 14 December 2000, and *Order on ARR & Tariff for Distribution and Retail Supply*, 22 December 2000.

———, Consultation Paper II—*Issues of Tariff Philosophy*, Panchkula, Haryana, 1999.

Haryana State Electricity Board, *Annual Statement of Accounts and Annual Administration Reports*, various issues, Panchkula, Haryana.

Jain, Neeraj, *Globalisation or Recolonisation*, Pune: Elgar, 2001.

Jyoti, Bhattacharya, Kankar Reddy, B. Sudhakar and K.S. Parikh 'Energy Systems: Need for New Momentum', in Kirit S. Parikh, ed., *India Development Report 1997*, IGIDR, New Delhi: Oxford Univresity Press, 1997, pp. 77–94.

Kahn, Edward, *Electricity Utility Planning and Regulation*, Berkeley: Energy Research Group, University of California, 1991.

Kahn, Edward and Richard Gilbert (eds.), *International Comparisons of Electricity Regulation*, New York: Cambridge University Press, 1996.

Kannan, K.P. and N. Vijayamohanan Pillai, 'Plight of Power Sector in India-I: Physical Performance of SEBs', *Economic and Political Weekly*, vol. 36, no. 2, 13–19 January 2001, pp. 130–9.

———, 'Plight of Power Sector in India-II: Financial Performance of SEBs',

*Economic and Political Weekly*, vol. 36, no. 3, 20–6 January 2001, pp. 234–6.

Kodwani, Devendra G., 'Economic Regulation of Utility Industries', *Economic and Political Weekly*, vol. 35, no. 30, 22–8 July, pp. 2657–62.

Kumar, Surinder, 'Financial Performance and Pricing Policy: Haryana and Punjab Electricity Undertakings', *Institute of Public Enterprise (IPE) Journal*, vol. VII. no. 7, July–September 1985, Hyderabad.

———, 'Estimating Marginal Cost Price Structure: Haryana Electric Power System', *Energy Management*, vol. XXII, no. 2, New Delhi: National Productivity Council, 1988.

———, 'Energy in India's Economic Development: Emerging Issues in Electricity Policy', in G.K. Chadha (ed.), *Sectoral Issues in the Indian Economy: Policies and Perspectives* (Essays in Honour of Professor G.S. Bhalla), New Delhi: Har-Anand Publishers, 1994, pp. 177–92.

———, '*Power Sector' Alternative Economic Survey 1993–4*, New Delhi: Public Interest Research Group, 1994.

———, 'State Subsidisation and Pricing Policy in Electricity Supply: A Case Study of Haryana State', *Indian Journal of Power and River Valley Development*, vol. 59, no. 3&4, March–April 1999, Calcutta, pp. 29–39.

Kumar, Surinder and Vinod Kumar, *Electricity Theft and Conservation of Power* (PSEB sponsored project report), Chandigarh: Institute of Development and Communication, 1996.

Mehta, Abhay, *Power Play*, New Delhi: Orient Longman, 1997.

Morris, Sebastian, 'Regulatory Strategy and Restructuring: Model for Gujarat Power Sector', *Economic and Political Weekly*, vol 35, no. 23, 3–9 June 2000, pp. 1915–29.

———, 'Political Economy of Power Sector in India', *Economic and Political Weekly*, vol. 31, no. 21, 18–25 May 1996, pp. 1274–86.

National Council of Applied Economic Research, *Economic and Policy Reforms in India*, New Delhi, ADB-NCAER Project, 1999.

National Productivity Council, *Report on Review of Power End-Use Efficiencies*, New Delhi, 1991.

Nayyar, Deepak, *Economic Liberalisation in India: Analytics, Experience and Lessons*, Calcutta, Orient Longman, 1996.

Punjab State Electricity Board, *Report of the Comptroller and Auditor General for the year ending 31 March 1992*, Chandigarh, 1995.

———, *Sales Manual*, Patiala, 1995.

———, *Annual Administration Report*, and *Annual Statement of Accounts*, various years, Patiala.

———, *Energy Statistics of Punjab as on 31.3.1995*, Partial.

Purakayastha, P., 'New Power Policy: Bankrupting the Power Sector', *Economic and Political Weekly*, vol. 28, no. 20, May 1993, p. 955.

Purkayastha, Prabir and Arun Ghosh, *Current Power Sector Policies: A*

*Need for a National Debate*, New Delhi: National Working Group on Power.

Rao, M. Govinda, K.P. Kalirajan and S. Hand Ric, *The Economics of Electricity Supply in India*, New Delhi: Macmillan India, 1998.

Reddy, Amulya Kumar N. and Gladys Sumuttra, 'Integrated Resource Planning', *Energy for Sustainable Development*, vol. 3, no. 6, March 1997, Bangalore, pp. 14–16.

Reddy, Amulya K.N. et al., 'Development Focussed: End-Use-Oriented Electricity Scenario for Karnataka' I & II, *Economic and Political Weekly*, vol. 26, nos. 14 & 15, 6 and 13 April 1991.

Reddy, Amulya K.N., 'California Energy Crisis and the Lessons for Power Sector Reforms in India', *Economic and Political Weekly*, vol. 36, no. 18, May 2001, pp. 1533–40.

Sahota, Gian Singh, *Economic and Fiscal Gains from Liberalisation in Punjab*, Institute for Development and Communication, Monograph Series III, New Delhi: Ajanta Publisher.

Sant, Girish and Shantanu Dixit, 'Beneficiaries of IPS Subsidy and Impact of Tariff Hikes', *Economic and Political Weekly*, vol. 31, no. 51, 21–8 Dec. 1996, p. 3315.

Sant, Girish and Shantanu Dixit, 'Least Cost Power Planning: Case Study of Maharashtra State', *Energy for Sustainable Development*, vol. 4, no. 1, June 2000, pp. 113–28.

Shankar, T.L., *Fiscal Impact of Electricity Boards Overdues on State's Finances*, Hydrabad: Administrative Staff College of India, 2001.

Swamy, Dalip S., *The Political Economy of Industrialization: From Self-Reliance to Globalization*, New Delhi: Sage Publishers, 1994.

Tata Energy Research Institute, *Teri News Wire*, various issues.

Upadhayay, Anil Kumar, 'Power Sector Reforms: Indian Experience and Global Trends', *Economic and Political Weekly*, vol. 35, no. 12, 18–24 March 2000, pp. 1023–8.

# Index